GW00319722

Windows Phone
Put people first.

Get local tog

🏠 Bing Local Scout only on Windows® Phone. Get the local low-down near you, wherever you are.

More from Bing on Windows Phone

♪ Find that killer track in one click with **Bing Music**.

◉ **Bing Vision** translates that foreign sign or menu for you.

🎤 Text, call and search hands-free with **Bing Voice**.

Discover more at windowsphone.co.uk

Microsoft®

Contents

Welcome to Windows Phone

Although it's been around for only a comparatively short time, Windows Phone has already become a major player in the smartphone market, thanks to Microsoft's reputation, the operating system's simplicity and the range of phones available for it.

We've created this guide to show you how good Windows Phone is – from its music and video apps and photography features to its integration with other Microsoft services such as Office 365 and Xbox LIVE.

We've tested some of the best phones on the market, including Nokia's low-cost Lumia 710, up to the Lumia 900 and HTC Titan, which both have huge screens for watching videos and browsing the web.

Inside you'll find some of our favourite tips and tricks to help you get more from your Windows Phone, whether you're a novice setting up your device for the first time or a more experienced user who'd like to use a phone as an Xbox 360 remote control.

You'll find dozens of tips and recommended apps throughout the book, so whether you're looking for a way to check Facebook when you're out and about or you'd like some tips on saving battery life, you'll find it here.

If you're considering moving to Windows Phone – or you've just bought a new handset and want to find out more about it – this guide is for you.

Clare Hopping, Editor

Chapter 5

Xbox LIVE

Chapter 6

Out and about

Chapter 7

Photography

Chapter 8

Work smarter with your Windows Phone

Chapter 9

Other resources

people

recent

Charlotte Weiss

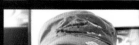

Chapter 1

What is Windows® Phone?

Everything at your fingertips

Windows® Phone arrived on the smartphone market in 2010, following on from Microsoft's previous mobile operating system, called Windows Mobile.

Windows Phone reinvented the whole concept of the smartphone. Rather than including a complicated or messy user interface, it brought in a completely new approach, ensuring everything you could ever want appears on the Start screen, with Live Tiles showing you all the latest information.

Navigation is easy. Windows Phone allows you to find your way around your phone with swipes and flicks. To access your installed applications, just swipe the screen and a list of your apps will appear. When you're

What are Live Tiles?
Live Tiles are square or rectangular tiles that sit on your Start screen and change according to what's going on. For example, Email will change when you receive a message, while the People Tile will flip and change when your closest contacts update a status on one of their social networks. You can 'pin' friends to the Start screen, ensuring all your information, the apps you use most and favourite people are right in front of you as soon as you unlock your phone.

in an app – such as Xbox LIVE, for example – you can swipe to view more information. It's all super-intuitive, and a big step on from the clunky Windows Mobile interface.

People are at the centre of your Windows Phone, and keeping in contact with those most important to you is more seamless than you've ever probably experienced before. You can pin your best friends to your Start screen, view a friend's social-networking life with just one tap and instantly call or text them with the touch of a finger.

We'll go over most of the details throughout this book, but to give you a little background, first we'll explain exactly where Windows Phone came from.

How Windows Phone has evolved

Believe it or not, Microsoft first started researching into a mobile operating system in 1990, when mobile phones were the size of bricks and couldn't really be used outside of a car because of the amount of battery power required.

The company first launched a mobile operating system in 1992. Called Windows CE, it was discontinued in 1995.

Pocket PC 2000, powered by Windows CE 3.0, was announced in 2000 and was the first 'real' mobile operating system. The platform appeared on Pocket PC hardware, Palm-size PC and Palmtop devices, and supported very few features compared to today's smartphones.

The follow-up, Pocket PC 2002, was the first Windows OS available for smartphones, and bridged the gap between

Pocket PCs and smartphones, which later merged into one style of mobile device.

The first version of Windows Mobile was launched in 2003. This first iteration came in four different flavours, each of which supported different features, designed to suit the hardware and use of each particular device. For example, Professional Edition was for budget Pocket PC touchscreen devices, while Premium Edition

Left to right:
HTC Titan
HTC Radar
Nokia Lumia 710
Nokia Lumia 800
Nokia Lumia 900

February 2010
- Windows Phone officially launched at Mobile World Congress 2010

October 2010
- First Windows Phone devices launched in Europe; hardware partners announced as HTC, Samsung, Dell and LG
- HTC Trophy, Mozart, HD7, LG Optimus 7, Samsung Omnia 7 revealed

November 2010
- Dell Venue Pro announced

January 2011
- HTC 7 Pro arrives

February 2011
- No-Do and Mango updates announced
- Microsoft and Nokia team up, promising cheaper Windows Phone phones

April 2011
- Mango update officially announced

October 2011
- HTC Titan and Radar released

March 2011
- First major Windows Phone update, No-Do, released

November 2011
- Nokia Lumia 710, Lumia 800 and Samsung Omnia W revealed

December 2011
- ZTE Tania announced

February 2012
- Tango update announced at Mobile World Congress, allowing lower-priced Windows Phones
- Nokia Lumia 610, 900 and ZTE Orbit revealed

had more features for business and enterprise users.

The next version of the operating system, Windows Mobile 5, was announced in 2005. It featured only a handful of minor improvements and was followed in 2007 by Windows Mobile 6. This version came in three editions: one for smartphones, one for Pocket PCs without a phone connection and one for Pocket PCs with a cellular connection.

2008's Windows Mobile 6.1 brought in a redesigned Start screen UI on smartphones, making it much more similar to the smartphones we've come to expect today.

Windows Phone 6.5 was a halfway point between Windows Mobile and Windows Phone. It was much more consumer-friendly, but not as intuitive as Windows Phone, which finally arrived on the scene in February 2010.

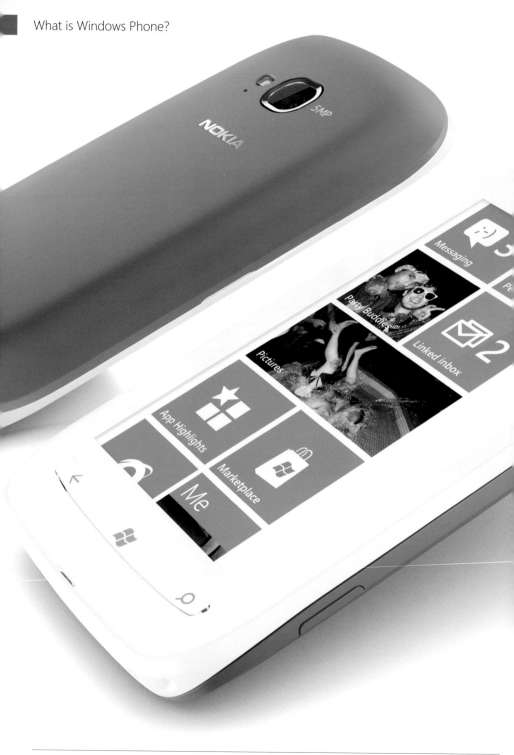

Nokia Lumia 710

The Nokia Lumia 710 is positioned at the budget end of Nokia's lineup – at least until the arrival of the Lumia 610, which hadn't launched at the time of writing. There's no curved display or laser-crafted unibody, for instance, but the back panel comes in a variety of different colours, which you can collect to customise your phone with. It's a nice touch and one younger users are sure to appreciate.

The Lumia 710 feels very lightweight in the hand, probably on account of its plastic chassis, and sports an impressive 3.7-inch ClearBlack (480x800 pixels) display that has a pixel density of 252ppi, which is very impressive for a mid-market phone such as this.

A microUSB, 3.5mm jack and Power/Unlock button run across the top of the device, and there's a volume rocker and camera shutter key on the right-hand side of the handset.

The Lumia 710's LCD display isn't quite as impressive as the AMOLED one on the Lumia 800 (see over), but it's still a massive improvement compared to earlier Windows Phone devices.

Nokia hasn't cut any corners in the hardware department either, fitting the Lumia 710 with a 1.4GHz Qualcomm MSM8255 Snapdragon chipset, 512MB of RAM, 8GB of storage, and a 5-megapixel camera with an LED flash and a 28mm f/2.4 lens.

The Lumia 710's imaging capabilities are easily on a par with many of last year's Windows Phone 7 flagship devices, but perhaps that isn't surprising: Nokia knows how to make a decent camera.

The company has managed to sneak in Nokia Maps, Nokia Drive and Nokia Music to help separate the Lumia range from the rest of the Windows Phone pack. What these applications do is pretty self-explanatory, but they do add significant value and utility to the handset.

We seriously rate the Nokia Lumia 710. If you're looking for a Windows Phone 7 handset but don't want to pay premium prices, this could very well be the phone you're looking for. ∎

★ Highlights

- Lightweight chassis
- Reasonably priced
- Removable battery

★ Top Tip

To share and tag pictures with Windows Phone, tap the Share on Facebook option from the photo's menu, add a caption and tag your friends until your heart's content.

★ Top Tip

Auto-fix corrects pictures if the lighting is wrong or they need sharpening. Tap the auto-fix option from the photo's options and it will magically correct itself.

Nokia Lumia 800

The Lumia 800 has effectively borrowed the Nokia N9's design, which means you get the same excellent build quality and great black, pink or blue rubbery plastic finish, making it very comfortable to hold.

The Lumia 800 feels great in the hand, largely because of its superb design. It weighs just over 140 grams, and is the first Windows Phone device that could reasonably be compared to the iPhone. The minimalist design and thoughtful layout is clearly the work of a company that pays attention to the details, much like Apple.

Under the hood, the Lumia 800 has a 1.4GHz Qualcomm Snapdragon processor and an Adreno 205 GPU. Nokia has bucked the current trend towards dual-core processors, and with good reason. Combined with 512MB of RAM, it's a very fast smartphone.

The 3.7-inch screen is small compared to the Lumia 900's giant 4.3-inch display (see over), but the 800's it still looks stunning. The curved glass makes it usable in the sun – a problem on many smartphones – and the AMOLED technology brings the operating system to life. To date, it's the best screen we've seen for Windows Phone.

Details using the Carl Zeiss lens and 8-megapixel camera are accurate, as are colours. Even when you transfer your photos to a computer and zoom in, you'll have to try hard to find many flaws.

The Lumia 800 comes with 16GB of storage, which is ample for the average user but not if you are used to lugging your entire music collection around with you. There's no microSD card slot, either, as is the trend across WP devices.

It may not be a dual-core monster, but that doesn't prevent the Windows Phone platform being blissfully easy to use. To not give it a chance is a great shame, as the pros really do outweigh the cons.

Perfect it isn't, but lovable it most certainly is. The Lumia 800 should be considered if you want to see what Windows Phone is about, especially as the handset is available for a shade under £400. ■

Highlights
- High-quality design
- 16GB internal storage
- Stunning screen

Top Tip
Facebook photos will be automatically filed in the same albums as in your profile, and you can add friends' photo albums to the People folder in the Pictures hub, too.

App Showcase
PhotoFunia allows you to edit pictures to your heart's content. Add pop art, lomography and vintage effects in a couple of clicks, and then save it to the cloud.

Nokia Lumia 900

T he Nokia Lumia 900 feels noticeably bigger in the hand than the Lumia 800, and it's also well designed. In fact, it's one of the few phones we can spot from a mile away in a sea of Android lookalikes.

The Lumia 900 also runs the equally pretty Windows Phone 7 operating system, with its Metro UI. With contrasting colours, Live Tiles and an incredibly easy-to-navigate interface, the phone ought to be a winner.

The Lumia 900's curvy, polycarbonate body looks just as nice as it feels. At the front of it, you'll find Nokia's 4.3-inch ClearBlack AMOLED display. What does that mean? Well, it means blacks actually look black, and colours are vibrant. The screen also has great contrast overall.

One side has a volume rocker, sleep/power button and a camera button. The other side is clean. At the top you'll find a mini-USB port and 3.5mm headset jack alongside a slot for the microSIM card. The bottom has a tiny grille to conceal the speaker and microphone. Inside, the Lumia 900 has a speedy 1.4GHz processor.

Nokia's N8 had a great camera, as did several of the company's other phones. The Lumia 900, like the Lumia 800, boasts an 8-megapixel camera with Carl Zeiss lens.

The UI is pretty and easy to navigate, making most things easy to figure out at a glance. You can trigger the snapper right from the Start screen as you can on other Nokia Lumia phones, allowing you to get creative the second you want to take a shot. You can use the same hardware button to take a photo, or tap the screen to focus and close the shutter.

There are also a range of manual settings, such as white balance and ISO, and a selection of different camera modes, such as macro mode.

The Lumia 900 is the star of the Windows Phone lineup. With its huge, bright, crystal-clear screen, speedy interface and top-quality mobile camera, we like it a lot. ■

Highlights

- Massive screen
- Great camera
- Fast processor

Top Tip

As well as displaying your contacts' social feeds, People Hub also lets you view, comment on and tag friends' photos. Just tap on People>All>Select a contact>Pictures.

App Showcase

Fantasia Painter Free is a free painting app for Windows Phone. It comes with lots of effects and strokes you can use to create your artistic masterpieces.

HTC Radar

Not everyone wants a giant display on their phone; smaller can be more beautiful, particularly when it comes to mobiles. HTC obviously had this in mind when it released the Radar alongside the huge HTC Titan (see over).

The Radar isn't that much smaller than the Titan – it's more a turbocharged version of a previous HTC handset, the Trophy – but a 3.8-inch display makes it easier to pocket and hold in one hand. The screen may be smaller than the Titan's, but the 480x800-pixel resolution ensures detail is maintained.

Internally, the Radar has a 1GHz processor; nothing special in a world of dual-core processors, but Windows Phone is designed to glide at lower speeds, and it certainly does that. You can jump into apps and games quickly, and scrolling up and down the Start screen is always effortless and slick.

Windows Phone Mango makes using the Radar easy. Enter your Hotmail, Facebook and Twitter details, and all your contacts from each are pulled in. Photos from Facebook can be stored on your phone, too.

A 5-megapixel camera provides ample quality for taking photos when out and about. Images are relatively noise-free and detailed. 720p video ensures any footage you record is also going to be of good quality.

On the outside, the Radar is constructed using a unibody aluminium shell, which gives it a feeling of quality. This is a high-end device, after all, and so it's important to get that feeling when using it. It's fairly light and the rounded edges make it easy to grip. The smattering of grey finishes off a smart-looking device.

There's no support for microSD cards, but 8GB of storage and 25GB from Microsoft's SkyDrive service should provide ample space. You may need to be just a tad more selective than you would with a 16GB or 32GB device.

As the Radar is an HTC device, it comes with a number of HTC-specific apps, such as a sound equaliser app and one for checking shares. These are nice extras, especially when it means you can enable SRS surround sound, and worth using.

Ultimately, the HTC Radar is a capable device with a stylish exterior. It's very fast, too, which makes using Windows Phone is a joy.

Throw in its cheaper price and the HTC extras, and the end result is a fine Windows Phone Mango smartphone capable of keeping you in touch with friends and family without making life difficult. ■

★ Highlights

- High-quality camera
- Attractive design
- Reasonably priced

Top Tip

Long-press the back key to enter multitasking mode. From here, you can switch between apps effortlessly.

App showcase

The SkyDrive app on Windows Phone allows you to access all your files in one well-designed place.

HTC Titan

T he name 'Titan' implies something fairly big, and this Windows Phone device has a huge 4.7-inch display and a powerful 1.5GHz processor, which means it's more than well equipped for any task.

Continuing in the large trend is an 8-megapixel camera with a dual-LED flash; a powerful combination. The Titan also has a front-facing camera for video calls.

All that hardware obviously has to go somewhere, but the Titan isn't actually that chunky, and will fit into your pocket nice and easily.

A large screen is only really useful when the operating system it displays looks good, and Windows Phone certainly doesn't disappoint. In Mango form, it's incredibly easy to use and stylish. The Live Tiles look even larger on a big display, too, making them easier to read at a quick glance.

The Titan can multitask simply by holding the back button, and built-in functionality such as Bing means you can find local restaurants or whatever you want just by pressing a button.

You also have access to the Windows Phone Marketplace's 80,000 apps, which means you can download the likes of Angry Birds, Facebook and Twitter with little effort.

Thanks to the 1.5GHz processor, the Titan is a very powerful handset and one that will be able to handle everything you throw at it.

The Titan excelled in our photography and video tests. Images look clear and bright, without being noisy. Video quality is also good for those moments when a picture isn't enough - we're talking 720p, to be precise. Rounding off the imaging options is a dedicated button for starting the camera, so you can go straight from the lock screen to photo-ready in seconds.

Some HTC phones, such as the Desire HD, have had issues with battery life, but the Titan's size allows it to have a larger battery. This means it can last a day before you'll need to give it some more juice.

Windows Phone doesn't have a smartphone with such a large display, which makes the Titan something of a rarity, and we like that. The operating system really stands out on all 4.7 inches of the display, and games, movies and films really have that much more impact.

The Titan might not be as portable as some of its smaller-screen counterparts, but Windows Phone really doesn't have the same presence on any other device, which makes the Titan special. ∎

Highlights
- Huge display
- Great battery life
- Fast processor

Top Tip

Press and hold any of the Live Tiles on the Start screen to enter edit mode. Here, you can move tiles around or delete them altogether.

App Showcase

The Metro app is a great way to get your daily news on the go. It's split into categories, each of which can be pinned to your Start screen.

Chapter 2

Getting the most from your Windows Phone

I f you're thinking of moving from another smartphone platform, you'll quickly notice how Windows Phone is very different from the off. It has a simple interface and the ability to customise the Start screen as you wish, without it looking cluttered.

If you're moving from a non-smartphone, you'll find things are more interactive, more feature-packed and more exciting, but not complicated, which is why Windows Phone is perfect for novice users.

In this chapter, we'll show you how to get the most from your new phone, whether you

want to know how to set it up or you simply want to start downloading and installing apps straight away.

Once you've been using Windows Phone for a while, the tips and tricks section at the back of this chapter will show you how to get more from the platform.

Your first 15 minutes

When you first turn on your Windows Phone smartphone, you'll be guided through how to set up and use the device, whether you're using a Nokia, HTC or Samsung handset. Just in case you need a nudge along the way, though, here's a quick guide to getting up and running with Windows Phone.

Before you do anything, ensure you charge your Windows Phone for at least six hours, if not overnight. This will make your phone's battery last longer in the long run.

After you've charged your new device, turn it on. You'll immediately be greeted by the Welcome screen. From here, click on Get started and select your language.

You'll have to accept the Windows Phone conditions before you can continue any further. You can view these by tapping on Windows Phone Terms of Use.

Now you can select how you want to configure your Windows Phone. There are two options: Recommended, which will enable your mobile data and send phone

usage information, keyboard touch information and problems reports to Microsoft automatically. This is designed to help the company with updates to the platform.

The other option is Custom. Here you can change how information is sent to Microsoft or prevent mobile data usage.

Once you've chosen how you want to set up your phone, choose your time zone. You'll then be asked either to enter your Windows Live ID login details, or to create a Windows Live ID if you don't already have one.

Windows Live allows you to access Microsoft services, including Xbox LIVE, Zune and Marketplace. If you already have a Zune, Hotmail or Xbox account, you can use this ID.

After you've set up your Windows Live account, you may be asked to accept the phone manufacturer's terms and conditions.

Once that's done, you're ready to start customising your phone's Start screen and set up email and social-networking accounts. You can also now start installing apps from the Windows Marketplace.

The basics: Live Tiles

Live Tiles are essentially what brings a Windows Phone to life. They sit on the Start screen and flip and move as soon as anything changes – whether you receive a new email or text message, or one of your contacts updates their social feeds.

You can also set up Live Tiles for many of the apps available from the Windows Marketplace. Our favourite is the Accuweather application, which will change according to the weather in your particular location. If it's raining, for example, the picture will display storm clouds, along with the temperature, which changes in a similar way.

We'll explain more about how to add new Live Tiles and move them around the Start screen on page 27.

Top Tip

If you've downloaded an app that supports Live Tile mode and you want to activate it, you'll find the option to turn it on or off in the app's Settings menu.

The basics: Email

Microsoft's mobile operating system offers unbeatable integration with email. Windows Phone devices support a whole range of email clients, including Windows Live, Gmail, Yahoo and Exchange. We've explained a little more about email in chapter 8, but here's how to set up your email.

■ Head to the Settings menu from the applications list (swipe from right to left from the Start screen to find this), and then select email+accounts

■ Tap on the plus icon (+) to add an account
■ Choose which kind of email your account is. If your email supplier isn't listed, select Other account. Chances are that if you're trying to set up a work email account, you'll need to select Outlook, which is Exchange email
■ Now you'll need to enter your email account details, including your email address and password
■ Some email accounts may struggle to find all the

details required from just your email address, so you may need to add in the domain and server. You can find out these details from your IT department or email provider if you're unsure
■ Once you've set up your email account, it will synchronise all emails to your phone. You can choose to sync other information, such as calendars and contacts, by selecting the account from the email+accounts menu and tapping the tickboxes.

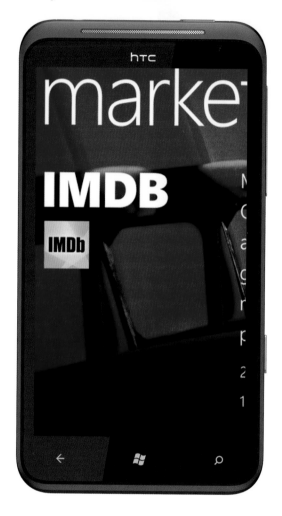

The basics: Apps and the Marketplace

O nce you've set up your phone's Start screen with Live Tiles and email, you'll want to start downloading apps, making the most of the selection available from the Windows Marketplace.

When you head to the Marketplace from the apps list, you'll first see the featured application, with the background an image to match. Swipe your finger from right to left, where you can choose between applications, games and music. If you want to search for a particular app, tap the search icon and suggestions will pop up.

The next screen will show you a selection of recommended apps, while another displays recommended games. The final screen in the Marketplace is music recommendations.

Once you've found an app you think you'd like to download, tap on its icon to read more details about it, plus the pricing information. If it's free, you can just tap to download. If a price is

displayed, you can download
a trial first to try before you buy.

However, before you
can download a paid-for
application you'll have to set up
an account. To do this, choose
your country, enter your date of
birth and select the 'personalise
my music' box if you wish to
send your music information

to Microsoft. This means
that in future you will see
recommended artists for you
to download on Zune. Accept
the terms and conditions and
you'll be provided with an
Xbox GamerTag, which can be
changed in the Games Hub.

Now you're ready to start
downloading applications. If

you choose a paid-for app
you'll be asked for payment,
so make sure you have a
credit or debit card ready.

Once you've entered your
payment details, the app will
download to your phone. You'll
see its download or installation
status in the Apps screen, or
the Games Hub if it's a game.

The basics: Customising your phone

Windows Phone is designed to be personal. You can make the Start screen appear exactly as you want it by pinning photos, websites, apps or anything else to it. You can also add your own photos as wallpaper on the lock screen, change the colour of the tiles and the background and have all your favourite contacts just a tap away. Here we show you how

To pin an app to the Start screen:
- From Start, flick left to the Apps list
- Tap and hold the App you want and tap Pin to Start.

To pin a website:
- Open the website you want
- Tap More, then Pin to Start

To pin a location:
- From Start, flick left to the Apps list, then tap Maps
- Type the location you want
- Tap the flag on your location, then tap Pin.

To unpin a tile:
- Tap and hold the unwanted tile
- Tap Unpin.

To change accent colour:
- From Start, tap the arrow to go to the Apps list, then tap Settings
- Tap Theme
- Tap Accent Colour list
- Tap the colour you want. You can check out your new theme colour in the highlight sentence. You'll see your accent colour in places such as tiles, web links, and your Apps list.

To change the background theme:
- From Start, tap the arrow to go to the Apps list, then tap Settings
- Tap Theme
- Tap Background list
- Tap Dark to make your background black
- Tap Light to make your background white

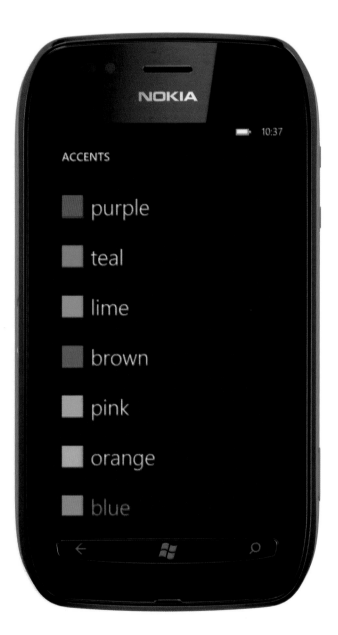

The basics: Settings

The Settings menu on your Windows Phone allows you to customise your phone, manage applications and change how it works. Here's a guide to what you'll find on the System menu

Ringtones+sounds This is where to change your ringtone

Theme The place to go to change the background and foreground colours

Flight mode When activated, Flight mode disables all connections – ideal for a plane or at the theatre, for example

WiFi This is where you set up and manage Wi-Fi connections

Bluetooth To activate, connect and change the name of your Bluetooth connections

Email+accounts Set up your Facebook, Twitter, LinkedIn and email accounts here

Lock+wallpaper Here you can change the wallpaper, alter how long the screen is turned on before it goes into standby mode, set a password and turn on the ability to show cover art when you're playing music

Location Enables and disables GPS and location services

Mobile network This is where to head if you want to turn the antenna off, turn roaming on and off, choose whether your phone can connect to 3G (high speed internet) and whether your phone automatically connects to a network. You can also add APNs in this menu

Battery saver This option allows you to adjust your phone's power settings and turn on battery-saver mode if you're running low on juice

Brightness Under this menu, you can decide how bright you want your screen. The brighter your screen, the faster your battery will run out

Keyboard Allows you to change the language of the keyboard

Region+language Where you change your country, language and how date/time is displayed

Ease of access This menu is for enabling TTY/TDD mode and speech-for-phone accessibility

Speech Here you can enable speech recognition and audio confirmations

Find my phone Once enabled this allows you to find your phone if it's lost or stolen on a map at windowsphone.com

Phone update Where you'll find any update notifications

About This is where you can find out about your phone's firmware version and where you can reset your phone

Feedback When enabled, this sends feedback to Microsoft to help improve Windows Phone

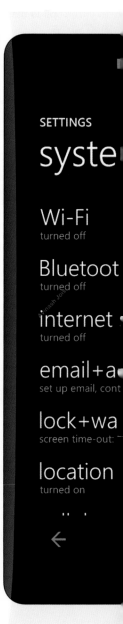

You can also adjust the behaviour of your apps in the Settings menu. Here's a quick rundown of the options

Background tasks This refers to the applications that can work in the background while you're looking at something else. You can choose to turn background activity on or off

Games This setting allows you to change how your phone connects with Xbox LIVE, including synchronising game requests, uploading achievements and profiles

Internet Explorer Here you can adjust your web browser's settings by turning cookies on and off, changing whether you want to get suggestions from Bing and choosing whether you want your browsing history kept. You can also choose where you want links to open and whether you would prefer sites to open in a mobile view or go straight to the desktop version of a website

Maps Here you change settings such as orientation and screen rotate while navigating

Messaging This option allows you to turn on Facebook chat, SMS delivery confirmation (network dependent) and Group text. Your SMS centre number is also displayed here

Music+Video Here you can opt to connect with Zune with access to your Zune settings

Office This section holds your Office username and enables you to turn on SharePoint and SharePoint settings

People This lets you import SIM contacts, filter your contact list and choose how you want names displayed in the contacts list. You can also add new accounts from here

Phone Displays your voicemail number, and from here you can choose to show your caller ID. You can also turn on or off the call forwarding, International assist and SIM security features here

Pictures+camera This section includes all your camera options. Here you can change things such as the option to take a photo when you touch the screen and whether you can press and hold the camera button to wake the phone. You can also prevent the camera launching accidentally when the phone is locked, include location information in pictures and upload all pictures automatically to SkyDrive. This is where you also nominate your Quick share account

Radio Set the default region for the radio app

Search This section includes location options, whether you can see the search button on the homescreen, whether you want Bing to suggest phrases when you start typing a search and whether you want Microsoft to store images from vision searches

Tips and tricks

Really want to master your Windows Phone? Discover the operating system's many talents with our insider's guide and you'll be an expert in no time

Use your Windows Phone as an Xbox 360 remote control
A free app available from the Windows Marketplace turns your Windows Phone into a remote control for your Xbox 360, so you can pause a movie on your Xbox, for example, using your mobile.

Called Xbox Companion, this handy app does all the hard work for you, so you can just sit back and relax.

■ First, head on over to the Windows Marketplace by clicking on the Marketplace button
■ If the app isn't featured, press the search button and type in Xbox Companion
■ Select the app and choose to install it

■ Once you've installed Xbox Companion, make sure your Xbox 360 is turned on and launch the app.
■ It will now look for your Xbox and try to connect to it. If it fails, just try again. Once connected, you'll see a load of options on how to control your Xbox 360 from your phone. Job done!

WANT TO KNOW MORE ABOUT SMARTPHONES AND TABLETS?

Check out **www.knowyourmobile.com** for buying advice plus
the latest news, reviews and comparisons so you can make
the right decision for your next gadget

App and game reviews	Comprehensive mobile glossary	How to guides for every mobile device

For everything mobile

Tips and tricks continued

How to set a lock screen password

Losing a mobile phone is something most of us have done at some point, and with most smartphones connected to a number of social networks, email accounts and so on as well as containing all your contacts, the loss goes further than just the handset itself.

Fortunately, Windows Phone can safeguard your phone should the worst happen. It can also prevent people from messing with your phone.

- From the main menu either swipe from right to left on the screen or press the right arrow button on the top right of the interface
- Scroll through the icons until you get to the Settings menu, and tap the icon
- From the list that appears, select Lock + Wallpaper
- Flick the Password setting toggle to the right to switch password mode on. The status should read 'On', and the toggle will fill with colour
- Tap on the Change Password button
- Enter a password. You can only enter numbers, and you will need to enter it twice. If you already have a password you will need to enter it first
- Press Done
- You can also set how often you want the phone to request a password – either each time you activate the homescreen or at timed intervals.

NOKIA

14:25

CHOOSE AN ITEM

each time

30 seconds

1 minute

3 minutes

5 minutes

15 minutes

30 minutes

Merging contacts

It's all too easy to end up with multiple contacts for the same person, each with different information. Windows Phone lets you merge these contacts together in order to keep your address book tidy.

This guide will work any Windows Phone device with Windows Phone Mango.

How to link a contact

- From the Start screen, tap the People tile
- You should be on the All section. If not, swipe across until you find it
- Select the contact you want to use as the main contact for that person
- Press the link icon – it resembles a chain
- Select the contact to which you want to link from the list of suggestions. If the contact you want isn't there, tap Choose a Contact and manually select it from the address book.

How to unlink a contact

- In the People hub, select the main contact for the person you want to unlink
- Press the Unlink button - this will be a chain icon with a number above it, representing the number of other contacts linked to it
- Select the contact you wish to unlink from the list.

Tips and tricks continued

How to switch to desktop mode in Internet Explorer

If you want to view the full version of your favourite web page, rather than the scaled-down, data-friendly mobile version, you can turn on Desktop browsing by opening Internet Explorer and tapping on the more (...) key. Select Settings, and you can choose to view either the mobile or desktop version.

How to take pictures direct from the lock screen

If you see a photo opportunity and want to snap it without having to go through the rigmarole of unlocking your device and opening the camera app, simply hold down the camera button on your device for three seconds. You will then be able to take a photo without having to unlock your phone or enter your password.

How to multitask on Windows Phone

Like a number of smartphone platforms, Windows Phone supports multitasking, meaning you can quickly switch between apps. To go from one app to another, press the back button for slightly longer than usual, and you'll see the multitask view. Each of the open applications will display as a thumbnail. To open an app from the menu, just tap on the app's thumbnail.

How to import contacts from your SIM card to your Windows Phone

If you've saved all your contacts on a SIM card, you can import them to your Windows Phone very easily. To do so, follow these instructions:

■ From the Start screen, select People, and choose the Settings option
■ Select Import SIM contacts
■ Your contacts will now be transferred from your SIM card to your phone. We recommend you keep your numbers on the SIM card and the phone so that if you lose or change your phone, they'll still be available on the SIM card.

Chapter 3

That's entertainment

Microsoft Zune

Microsoft's Zune PC software is your one-stop shop for all your media needs – we're talking music, film, apps, games and podcasts. It's free to download and simple to use, giving you instant access to a sea of content via your PC, Windows Phone and Xbox.

Once installed on your PC, Zune will index all of your existing media into its library and track down all the missing artwork – and it does this in moments. Now you can view your music just as the artists' intended, complete with exclusive HD images and full track information. Gone are the days of 'Untitled Album' and 'Unknown Artists' – Zune gets all the information for you automatically.

But it doesn't end there. Zune is also a media server, allowing you to stream content from your PC around your home, and features access to Microsoft's Marketplace, from where you can download film, music, apps, games and podcasts. It will also sync wirelessly with your Windows Phone, ensuring your handset is always up to date with your latest downloads.

Need more media? That's simple: just head on over to the Zune Marketplace and there you'll have access to an entire universe of games and applications, as well as music, video and podcasts. Sign up to Microsoft's Zune Pass music subscription service and you'll get instant access, anytime, to over 11 million tracks on your PC, Windows Phone and Xbox console.

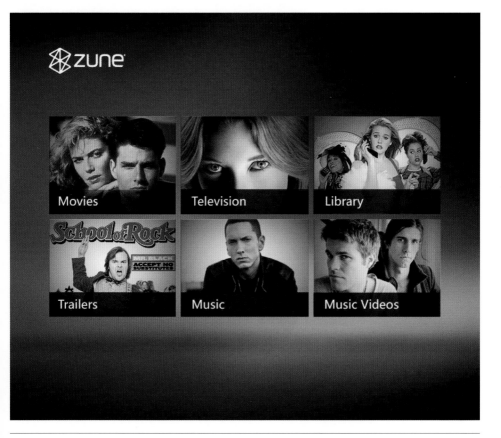

Music and video

You can think of the Music + Videos hub on your Windows Phone as a portable version of the Zune software on your computer. Inside the Music + Video hub you'll be able to access all your music, video and podcasts, as well as browse music using Microsoft's Zune Pass (although this requires a subscription; see opposite for more details) and see what you've recently been listening to via the History tab.

The Music + Video hub also enables you to create playlists, listen to FM radio broadcasts, subscribe to podcasts and download stuff from the Marketplace. But first things first – let's show you how easy it is to get music from your computer to your Windows Phone using Zune.

■ If you don't already have Zune installed on your PC, go to www.zune.net and download it
■ Once you've installed it, open Zune on your PC
■ Connect your Windows Phone to your PC with a USB cable
■ On your PC version of Zune, select Collections
■ You'll now be presented with four options: Music, Videos, Pictures and Podcasts
■ Select the category you want to synchronise with your phone
■ Now drag the selected items to the phone symbol in the bottom left-hand corner to begin the synchronisation process.

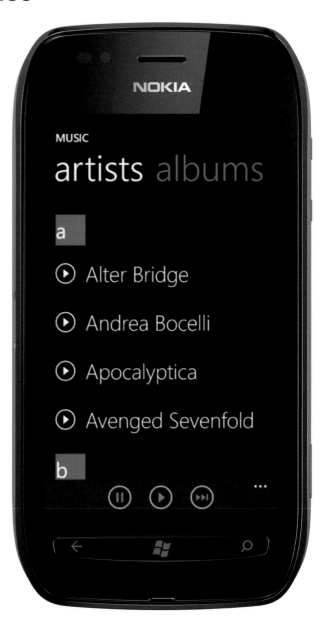

Changing options

If storage on your Windows Phone isn't an issue and you want to transfer all the music from your PC to your mobile device, you simply have to change the Sync Options. You can then include any new stuff as and when you download it. To do this with music tracks:

■ Go to the Settings option in Zune on your PC
■ Select Phone, then Sync Options
■ Go to Music and select All. Now connect your Windows Phone to your PC, and all your tracks will be transferred to your phone, including anything new that you download.

Wireless syncing

If you don't want to use a USB cable to get your media from your PC to your Windows Phone, setting up wireless syncing is simple:

■ First ensure that your Windows Phone and PC are connected to the same Wi-Fi network
■ Connect your Windows Phone to the PC via USB
■ In Zune, go to Settings, then Phone, and select Wireless Sync
■ Follow the on-screen instructions.

You will need to ensure that your Windows Phone has enough space available to sync your entire PC-based Zune library. If you're worried about using all your phone's memory, set up a memory reserve so you always have a spare gigabyte or two to play with:

■ Go to Settings, then Phone
■ Select Reserved Space
  Music + Video on your Windows Phone
  Once you've chosen your syncing options and transferred all the music and video content you want from your PC to your Windows Phone, it's time to start enjoying music and video while on the move.

For the ultimate Zune experience across all your Windows products, you can sign up for a Zune Pass. For £8.99 a month, this gives you access to over 11 million tracks and thousands of movies on your Windows Phone, PC and Xbox console. For further information about Zune Pass, visit tinyurl.com/zunepass1.

Radio

Your Windows Phone can do a lot more than just play MP3 music files and videos. It also has an FM radio, which means you can turn into your favourite radio stations while on the move – always handy when you're operating on a limited 3G connection.

Windows Phone's Music + Video hub lets you save your favourite stations to save you having to search for it every time you want to tune in. You can save as many stations as you like, too.

Note that you'll need the headphones that were supplied with your Windows Phone handset, as they also contain a radio antenna. Once you've plugged them in, it's simple to tune in:

- Open the Music + Video hub on your phone
- Flick across to Zune
- Select Radio
- To choose a station, flick from left and right (flicking, rather than swiping across the screen, takes you to stronger signals)
- Once you've found the station you're looking for, press Play.

Adding/removing favourites
Now you've located your desired radio station, saving it as a favourite so you can access it instantly in future couldn't be simpler:

- Simply tap on the Add Favourite option when you're on the desired station
- To remove a favourite, tap Remove Favourite.

Switching between speaker and headset modes
Listening to the radio via your headphones on the evening commute is a lot of fun – and it certainly helps pass the time. But once you're home, you can switch playback from your headphones to your Windows Phone's speaker seamlessly, so you won't miss a second:

- Whilst listening to a station, tap and hold the station number
- Select Switch to speaker or Switch to headset.

Podcasts

f you're not much of a radio fan but you prefer podcasts – or you like to listen to both – Windows Phone has that covered, too.

Subscribing to podcasts on Windows Phone can be done in two ways: either using the Zune software on your PC, or directly from the Marketplace application on your Windows Phone. Both options are simple; here we'll show you how to do it on your phone:

Subscribing to podcasts via your Windows Phone

- From the Start screen, go to the Windows Marketplace app
- Once inside the Marketplace, select Podcasts
- Now you can do one of two things: browse by category or search
- To browse the categories, flick from left or right
- To search, hit the Search key, type the name of the podcast, and hit Enter
- To read more information about the podcast – such as its subject matter, how long it lasts and who features, in it for example – simply swipe your fingers left or right
- Once you've found the podcast you want, select the Subscribe option
- Should you want to delete a podcast from your phone, simply hold down on it and select Delete.

Marketplace

Windows Phone
Put people first.

search applications and games

Discover Buy Marketplace How-to My Phone   Sign in

Applications Games

Marketplace

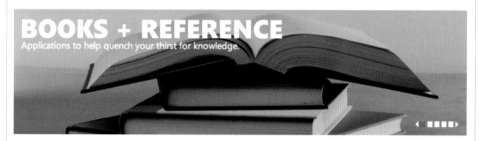

BOOKS + REFERENCE
Applications to help quench your thirst for knowledge.

Applications

Free **Top** New   All

Skype	Facebook	Adobe® Reader®	YouTube
★★★★	★★★	★★★	★★
Ratings: 557	Ratings: 3648		Ratings: 710

Games

Xbox LIVE Free **Top** New   All

Sid Meier's Pirates!	Civilization Revolution	iStunt 2	Gerbil Physics
★★★★	★★★★★	★★★★★	★★★
		Ratings: 213	Ratings: 42

Whatever you're into, there's something for you inside the Windows Marketplace. Whether it's music, films, applications, books or games that interests you, it's all on there.

You can access the Marketplace and browse its content either via the app installed on your Windows Phone or by pointing your web browser at windowsphone.com/marketplace.

If you access the Marketplace on your Windows Phone, you'll be able to browse and download a huge variety of games and music.

Visit the Marketplace on your Xbox, however, and you get instant access to almost any media content you could possibly think of, whether it's games, apps, movies or music. You can stream movies in high-definition 1080p format, listen to an unlimited number of tracks and albums using your Zune Pass and download and play thousands of available game titles.

The Zune Marketplace inside your PC's Zune software is the place to go for music and movies. From here you can rent, buy, download and stream thousands of movies and albums, as well as browse channels, playlists and tunes to your heart's content.

The truly great thing about Zune and its Marketplace is that once you've downloaded something, such as a movie or an album, it automatically becomes available on all your devices, including your Windows Phone. All you have to do is sync the device (see page 39) and, wherever you are in the world, you'll have access to all your media.

Headphones for music

Now that you've got to grips with Zune and filled your phone with music, you'll need some decent headphones so you can enjoy it all properly. But which set is right for you? We've lined up a trio of headphones that will appeal to everybody, even those on a strict budget

SoundMAGIC E10 £34.99 (amazon.co.uk)

Thanks to the 3.5mm jack socket, the E10s will plug into pretty much anything. The 1.4-metre cable gives you plenty of freedom without being too long and leading to tangles. There's also a handy movable clip attached to the cable, which lets you secure the headphones to your clothes, which is great when you're exercising, for example.

Sound quality is brilliantly sharp and bristling, with plenty of detail. So whatever you choose to put through the E10s, be it Mastodon or Wagner, the music sounds truly alive – just as the artists would have intended.

V-Moda Crossfade LP £102 (zazdas.com)

In terms of sound quality, the Crossfade headphones certainly do not disappoint. With an impressive frequency range of 5Hz to 30kHz, which is pumped into your head via the V-Moda's patented 'Dual Diaphragm' 50mm drivers, you need only a few seconds to realise this!

Weighing just 280g, these lightweight cans are comfortable to wear. If you listen to a lot of music when you're out and you need some headphones that do everything well, the V-Moda Crossfade LP set should be your first port of call.

Jabra Chill £8.50 (amazon.co.uk)

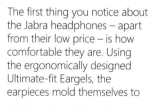

The first thing you notice about the Jabra headphones – apart from their low price – is how comfortable they are. Using the ergonomically designed Ultimate-fit Eargels, the earpieces mold themselves to contours of your ear to guarantee comfort.

Sleek, elegant and with a stylish black and grey finish, the Chill headphones also look great – even the gold-plated 3.5mm plug is pretty.

Bing Vision

Bing Vision is a kind of augmented reality on steroids. Imagine being able to translate entire pages of text simply by hovering your Windows Phone over it. There's no need to spend hours sifting through a book, translating signs, books and menus word by word – just let Bing do it for you.

Bing Vision also lets you scan objects, such as book covers, letting you compare prices and ensuring you always get the best deal. Simply point your Windows Phone at the object in question, wait for Bing Vision to kick in, then sit back and peruse the results.

And that's just the beginning of its capabilities. For instance, you can speak into Bing Vision and get it to repeat what you've just said in a variety of languages. To say Bing Vision makes a good travel companion would be an understatement – it's a godsend!

Another cool aspect of Bing Vision is its Newspaper match feature. Say, for example, you've just read an interesting article in The Times newspaper and you wanted to save it, or find out more information about the topic. Thanks to Bing Vision, you can take a picture of it with your Windows Phone and Bing will search online for electronic versions of that article and ones related to it using the physical newspaper's text and images. Clever, huh?

Bing Music

Having a passion for music is one thing, but knowing the name of every track that comes on the radio is quite another. In the past, finding out the name of a mystery song you love on the radio or TV could be quite tricky – well not anymore. Welcome to the world of Bing Music.

The next time you hear a song and you're not sure who it is, simply grab your Windows Phone, open Bing and hit the musical note symbol. Bing will then analyse the sound and determine the artist, the name of the track and the album it's from, along with lots more information about the artist.

Not only that, but once Bing has analysed the track it will locate it inside the Zune Marketplace, from where you'll be able to purchase or buy it instantly. Bing Music is a revelation – music discovery will never be the same again. Together with Windows Phone it will soon have you expanding you record collection.

Bing Voice

Search – both on your computer and your smartphone – is evolving. Microsoft knows this, and the company is redefining how people search and discover content on the web with Bing and its arsenal of tools.

One such tool is Bing Voice, which lets you search for things simply by speaking into your phone. So next time you're out and about and want to know something, simply open Bing, hit the Voice key, say something and watch the search results appear right before your eyes.

Bing Voice makes search so quick that you'll be making new discoveries faster than ever before. So say goodbye to typing and hello to complete freedom with Bing Voice.

Smart searching

All Windows Phone handsets come with Bing hardwired into them. That means the web is only ever one click away. However, Bing is way more than just a search engine – it's also a discovery tool that links you to the web and what's going on around you. It's the smarter way to make discoveries.

With Bing, less is more: it's all about quality ahead of quantity. So when you search for something – a coffee shop, say – you get not only the results that are relevant to your query, but Bing's Local Scout feature also provides those near to your current GPS position. This way you cut through the clutter and straight to the information you want.

You're not limited to typing to search, either. Your phone can read with Bing Vision, which uses your camera to scan books, DVDs, QR codes and barcodes. Bing can also tell the names of songs that you hear with Music, and thanks to Voice you can now just talk to your Windows Phone to get results.

You'll first have to turn on Use My Location in Settings to share your position and get access to what's going on around you. To use Local Scout, open Bing, search for, say, a local gastro pub, and Local Scout will show you all the gastro pubs near your current position, complete with reviews, contact details and directions.

Shopping apps

eBay

Once you've logged into your eBay account using this app, you're presented with just two screens – a search menu and MyEbay – from which to choose. The search screen is the landing page and comes with a selection of popular search terms with images for quick reference, while MyEbay displays any items you're watching, bidding and lots more bunched into a simple list.

After searching for a product you're presented with a number of swipeable screens covering auctions and Buy It Now offers. Each auction is displayed with the product picture, current bid, postage, number of bids and time remaining, with the auctions ending soonest appearing first. This can be customised using the toolbar, which also hides the useful 'refine' function, which lets you sort the wheat from the chaff.

Amazon

Amazon has everything you could ever wish for and much, much more. It seems that whatever you're looking for – no matter how obscure it is – Amazon has it. The Amazon Mobile for Windows Phone app lets you browse items, read reviews, compare prices, do One-Click purchasing just like you can on the web and a whole load more.

The latest version of the app – which, like all the other apps here, is available in the Marketplace – features barcode and QR scanning, so you can scan a physical object in a shop on the high street, and find out instantly if you can get it cheaper from Amazon.

The Amazon Mobile app for Windows Phone is beautifully presented and packed full of useful features. It's sure to take up a prime spot on your Start screen.

Groupon

If you don't know what Groupon is, where have you been? It's possibly the biggest thing to happen to the way people shop since Amazon first opened its virtual doors.

Groupon is a voucher service that gets subscribers anything from 50 to 90 per cent off a whole range of goods, services and produce. Now it's on Windows Phone you can catch up on the latest deals wherever you are.

Groupon for Windows Phone lets you redeem deals directly from your phone so you can purchase stuff while on the move. Best of all, it uses your GPS position to tell you how close you are to certain deals and offers. It's a must-have application for any urban dweller.

The app is simple to use, but you may get addicted to constantly checking out deals!

News apps

Engadget

Love your technology? Of course you do – you've got a Windows Phone. But to ensure that you're always up to date with the latest trends affecting the ever-changing tech world, be sure to download the Engadget application for Windows Phone.

Redesigned specifically for Windows Phone Mango, Engadget has a clear, easy-to-use interface and supports LiveTiles, so the latest headlines will appear dynamically on your Start screen. The app also supports social-networking integration with the likes of Facebook, Twitter, Tumblr, Evernote and Instapaper.

Engadget is jam-packed with reviews, regular news updates, masses of supplementary content, such as features and analysis, and some excellent video content to boot. It's an essential app for tech fans.

The Guardian

The Guardian is one the UK's most respected quality newspapers, and has been bringing readers news, sport, culture, business and technology for over 100 years. Now you can read it as an app on your Windows Phone.

Featuring a unique layout that lets you search for news by section, topic or contributor, alongside hours of award-winning video content and podcasts, The Guardian app for Windows Phone is one of the best and most accomplished news applications currently available, not to mention one of the most attractive.

Like other news apps, you can add The Guardian as a Live Tile to your Start screen for constantly updating news headlines, and select your favourite sections to ensure they're always available within a couple of taps.

Wonder Reader

Are you an information junkie who craves news piece after news piece and holds no allegiance to any one particular publication, instead preferring the four walls of your RSS feed? Join the club – RSS feeds are one of the best things to happen to the news.

If you're looking for a good RSS reader application, then look no further than Wonder Reader. Even if you're a complete novice in the world of RSS, it doesn't matter with Wonder Reader because it's so easy to set up and use. It also lets you share articles via Twitter, Facebook and email.

If you already use Google Reader for your RSS needs, you can simply connect Wonder Reader to your Google account and it will pull in all the feeds in a matter of seconds. There's never been an easier way to stay up to date.

Music apps

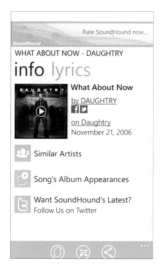

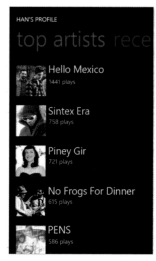

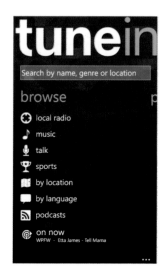

SoundHound

SoundHound is one of the most useful music apps we've discovered for Windows Phone, because it includes so much information.

First off, the app allows you to identify music, just like the better-known Shazam app.

However, once SoundHound has identified the tune playing, it lets you view the lyrics, share it on your social networks, download the tune or find out more about the artist. The application will even provide you with musical recommendations based on the tune you've just tagged.

If you're interested in what's happening in the music charts, you can check up on them here. You can also add your favourite tunes to your very own area, along with album art and much more.

What are you waiting for? Get wise with music now!

Last.fm

Pick any genre or artist, and Last.fm will play you tracks that are similar. As you hear new tracks, you can select songs as favourites or choose to ignore them, with the end result being a list of preferred tracks.

If you're already a Last.fm user, you can sync the app with your account, giving access to all your favourite radio stations, friends and tracks right from your Windows Phone.

If you add songs from your Windows Phone, these will be synced with your desktop account, meaning your music collection will be with you wherever you are.

Windows Phone users can enjoy the service for free, so there's no reason not to try Last.fm, as it's a great way of discovering new tracks and, with a great-looking UI, it's a seamless way of discovering and listening to new music.

TuneIn Radio

TuneIn Radio is the digital age's answer to radio. This free app gives you access to over 50,000 radio stations from around the world, with 1.2 million on-demand streams.

You can search for a specific radio station or pick one from a list. You can also search by the sort of radio show you are after, making it easy to find what you want to listen to.

TuneIn Radio supports the ability to listen to music while you're doing something else on your phone, so if you're checking email, playing a game or browsing the web, your favourite music can play in the background.

You can pin your top stations to the Start screen for one-tap playback, or add them to your presets for quick access.

Whatever you like listening to, TuneIn Radio has something for you.

Pinning apps to the Start screen

Unlike Android devices or the iPhone, Windows Phone's user interface is all about simplicity. Everything takes place over two screens – the Start screen and the Applications menu, which makes accessing anything you want a swift and painless process.

However, if you want even quicker access to your favourite applications, websites, games and searches, you can put them on the Start screen so they'll always be just a touch away. You can pin almost anything to the Start screen and, as we'll explain, it's extremely simple to do.

- Hold down on the item you want to pin to the Start screen
- When the option Pin to Start appears, tap it. The app will now appear on your Start screen
- If you want to move the app to a different location, go to the Start screen, hold down on the app and wait a moment. It should lift up, and you then can move it to wherever you want it.

Spotify

Spotify on your Windows Phone brings all the best of the music service to your mobile. If you're a premium Spotify user, you can listen to any track at any time, and also create playlists, just as you can on your PC.

Getting the most from mobile video

Your Windows Phone is more than just a phone. It's a mobile PC that connects to the web, a video player, an MP3 player and a phone, all in one. With Windows Phone there's no need to miss a thing. It lets you take all your music, videos and books with you wherever you go, so you're always connected.

There are a number of ways to enjoy mobile video on your Windows Phone. The first and most obvious method is via your Music + Video application, which contains all the videos you've shot using your Windows Phone's camera, as well as any movies that you've downloaded from the Marketplace.

The Music + Video hub splits all your video content into five sections: all, television, music, films and personal. It does this automatically, so you needn't worry about categorising everything. Just swipe from left to right to explore your Windows Phone's video collection.

You can move videos around between your PC and Windows Phone using Zune. Simply connect your Windows Phone to your PC and open Zune. Click the phone icon in the bottom left-hand corner and then select Video. You can now add or remove videos from your Windows Phone. To do this, follow these instructions:

- Connect your Windows Phone to your computer, either wirelessly or with a USB cable
- Open Zune on your PC
- Select Collection, and then Video
- Scroll down the list of videos until you see the one you want
- Drag the item to the phone icon in the lower-left corner of Zune
- The video will now sync to your Windows Phone.

Personal videos
Any pictures or videos you've shot using your Windows Phone will also be automatically synced to your PC when you connect to Zune. Simply go to Collection and then select Videos. Open My Video, and you'll see all the personal videos you've recorded using your Windows Phone.

Sharing your videos online
With Windows Phone you can share your videos on Facebook, Hotmail, Outlook, Gmail, and SkyDrive. All you need to do is go to Camera Roll, select the video you want to share, hit Options and click either Share to Facebook or Share... to access the other options.

Video apps

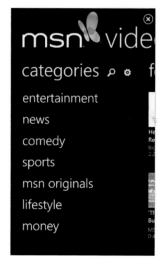

Netflix

Netflix is the biggest video-on-demand service in the US, and it's now available in the UK, bringing thousands of films, TV shows, cartoons and documentaries directly to your TV, Windows Phone, Xbox and PC.

You can rate your favourite programmes and films, and Netflix will recommend additional content for you to view. If you use the app on your Xbox, TV or PC, you can start watching on one device and then resume on another, without missing a second.

You'll need a Netflix account to use this app, which you can set up at the Netflix website at www.netflix.com/uk.

Once you've set up your account and downloaded the free Netflix app from the Marketplace to your phone, you'll be able to log in to Netflix on your mobile.

MSN Video

MSN Video is a free application that brings all the latest video content – including news stories, music videos, celebrity gossip and exclusive interviews – direct from the MSN network to your Windows Phone.

Open up MSN Video and you're presented with four categories: news, sport, entertainment, lifestyle and cars. Flick left and you're taken to the Featured videos section, which is full of the day's most popular videos.

The app will appear in your Music + Videos hub, allowing you to access all the videos you've previously watched.

You can share your favourite videos through Facebook or Twitter, and pin them to the Start screen for easy access.

Video content is displayed in full-screen mode, ensuring you don't miss out on any of the action.

YouTube Pro

YouTube Pro is a bigger and better version of the basic YouTube application on the Windows Marketplace, offering lots of UI tweaks and instant access to some of the best content available on the web's most popular video portal.

With YouTube Pro you can upload videos directly from your Windows Phone to your YouTube channel. Simply select the Uploading option, pick the video you want to share and sit back while it's uploaded to your YouTube channel.

If you lose your connection in the middle of uploading, watching or recording videos, the download will resume when you get the connection back, which is a particularly handy feature.

YouTube Pro is either available for free with ads, or without ads if you don't mind paying a small fee.

Essential apps

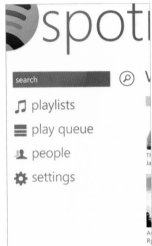

Skype

When you think of video calling, there's only really one company that comes to mind: Skype. Now owned by Microsoft, Skype is one of the best video-calling apps on the planet. You can use it on your PC, your TV and now on your Windows Phone.

Making video calls to other Skype users – be they Windows Phone users or PC users – is completely free. There's also the option to use Skype as an instant messenger (IM) client as well, which is great if you do lots of travelling or have friends that live abroad.

If you have friends or family that don't have a Skype account, you can call their mobile or landlines, too, providing you've purchased credit to do so.

The Skype app really is the best and easiest way to stay in touch wherever you are.

Spotify

If you love music, you probably already have a Spotify account. You can also get Spotify on Windows Phone, giving you access to tons of music while you're on the go. The Spotify app is free to download from the Marketplace, but you will need to be a premium subscriber to the service.

There are millions of tracks on Spotify's premium service, and no adverts to interrupt your listening pleasure. You can also listen to stuff when you're not online with Offline Mode.

Any playlists you make on your PC will be automatically made available on your phone and vice versa.

If you'd like to try the service before shelling out the full monthly fee, you can sign up to a 48-hour trial, which can be extended to a month if you follow the instructions on your sign-up email.

British Airways

Whether you're a frequent flyer or not, it's always handy to have a mobile application to check every last detail of your flight when you're travelling. The British Airways application for Windows Phone does just that, letting you keep tabs on check-in times, departure times and gate numbers.

It's a very comprehensive application and, because it's an official BA release, the information is always correct and bang up to date. The app also lets you view your BA boarding pass, track the departure and arrival of any British Airways flight and view maps of the terminal – always handy at Heathrow!

If you're part of the Executive Club, you can also get details of your points. As soon as you link the app with your account, it will automatically sync any upcoming flights.

Bing Translator

Navigating your way successfully around exotic cities and ordering food and supplies in a foreign tongue is usually something only seasoned travellers who are confident speaking a variety of languages will attempt. However, with the help of Microsoft's Translator app on your Windows Phone, you can feel at home and comfortable in your surroundings wherever you are in the world.

Bing Translator enables you to read, write and speak over 140 languages as if you knew them fluently. Using some of the best researchers and linguists on the planet, Microsoft has broken down and interpreted languages so now your Windows Phone can translate them into English, and vice versa.

Using Translator

Setting up and using Translator couldn't be easier.

- Once you've downloaded the app from the Marketplace, boot it up
- You'll now see a variety of options: Keyboard, Camera, Voice, Settings and Help. To get started, flick left to the Discover page and download a language pack – there's loads to choose from.

Text

You can point, scan and translate any text from one language to another. Whether it's a business card, a novel, a road sign or a menu – if it's written down, Translator will convert it. All you have to do is select the Camera option, point and the app will translate it into your specified language.

Type

What if you want to order a meal or tell a taxi driver where you want to go and you don't know the local lingo? Simple: open Translator, go to Type and enter the word, phrase or sentence you want converting and Translator will do the rest.

Click the audio symbol below the converted text to hear how the word, phrase or sentence is pronounced.

Voice

Translator's Voice option makes it even easier to convert what you're saying into another language. Simply go to the Voice option in Translator, say the phrase, word or sentence you want converting, and tap the speaker icon. Translator will now say the phrase back to you in your specified language; it's really that simple.

So the next time you're going aboard, you can leave that expensive phrase book on the shelves of the bookshop at the airport – Translator has got you covered.

Bing Get Me There

Whether you live and work in London, are visiting the capital for business or pleasure or you're on holiday in the Big Smoke, you need Bing's Get Me There app on your Windows Phone.

Get Me There is a travel app created exclusively for use in London. It's designed to get you from A to B in the quickest time possible by using a combination of live Tube and bus updates in conjunction with Bing Maps.

The result is a route that is tailored just for you based on up-to-the-minute travel information from London Underground, DLR and London's bus service providers. No other application available does this – not even the official Transport for London app.

Get Me There has a wealth of other features to help you find your way around the streets of London, and using it couldn't be simpler.

Adding favourites

If you're out and about in the city and you discover a nice restaurant, bar or coffee shop but it's not located in your usual haunts, you may be worried that in time you'll simply forget where it is. So what can you do?

Simple: just pin its location to your Windows Phone's Start screen using Get Me There. That way all you'll need to do to find it is tap the icon to get directions from your current position to the venue in question.

To do this, simply tap the Menu bar when you're at the location and add it to your favourites. Once it's saved to the Favourites

menu, hold down on it and select Pin to Start.

Live updates

Using public transport in London can be frustrating, and there's nothing worse than being stuck on a packed Tube. However, you can keep abreast of what's happening on the Underground via Get Me There's live Tube + Stations updates. This enables you to see if there are any delays on the line you want to take, and choose an alternative route.

Maps

Get Me There also comes with a Tube map, which as

well as helping you plan your journey also provides up-to-date information about any planned engineering works and which lines will be affected. In fact, there's so much information contained in this little Bing-powered application that you needn't fear going underground ever again.

Bing Get Me There makes travelling around London an absolute breeze. So whether you're a born and bred Londoner, a seasoned commuter or simply in the Big Smoke for a visit, Bing's Get Me There is an essential piece of kit for your Windows Phone.

Chapter 4

Keeping your social life under control

Keeping in touch

These days there seem to be a million and one ways to stay in touch with your friends and family, thanks to the rise of netbooks, tablets and smartphones. And with more and more people turning to social networks for their communicative fixes, keeping in contact with those you know has never been easier.

But what's the best way of reaching out to those around you? Facebook, Twitter, email, text messaging, Instant Messaging or a phone call?

The answer is simple: all of them. And with Windows Phone you can have them all – as well as phone calls and text messaging, it provides support for email, Facebook, Twitter, LinkedIn and Windows Live.

Windows Phone consolidates all your contacts, their social-networking profiles, email addresses, phone numbers and text messages into one place, making it easier than ever to stay in touch with your friends, family and colleagues.

At the centre of this organisation is Microsoft's People Hub. This is much more than a simple address book; it's your one-stop shop for all your social networking and messaging needs.

The future is about choice and better communication. With Microsoft's Windows Phone you'll always have both right at your fingertips. So whether you're addicted to Facebook, a serial tweeter or always on the lookout for new developments on LinkedIn, you'll find what you're looking for in the People Hub.

The People Hub

T he world seems to be getting smaller, thanks in part to the huge growth in popularity of social-networking sites such as Facebook, Twitter and LinkedIn. Billions of people all over the world now communicate online via one or more of the aforementioned social networks.

By introducing social-networking sites to your address book, Windows Phone's People Hub means you're no longer limited to contacting your friends and family via phone calls, text messaging or email; you can now keep in contact on Facebook, Twitter, Windows Live and LinkedIn.

Think of the People Hub as a futuristic address book. One that not only has all your existing contacts inside it, complete with a profile picture, phone number and email address, but also all their social-networking details as well.

The 'Me' section of the People Hub is all about you. Here you can post updates to your social-networking accounts, check in to Bing and Facebook Places, and view all your personal messages, comments and tweets.

Swipe left for the latest news from your contact's social networks in the 'What's New' section and left again to see the latest photo updates in 'Pictures.' It's all there, just as it would be on the Facebook or Twitter websites.

With tons of filtering results, the People Hub is also a great social feed reader, giving you up-to-the-minute updates from all your contacts. Interacting with content is extremely simple, too – just tap the update and the option to comment on it will appear.

There's a whole range of customisation options too, meaning you're always in control of what's going on inside your People Hub. Don't want to see Facebook results? Simple: just turn them off, and you'll only get updates from the sites you want.

The sky really is the limit with the People Hub. In this chapter we'll show you just how easy it is to stay on top of your social life with Microsoft's Windows Phone and its innovative People Hub.

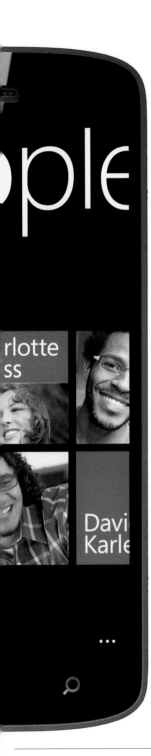

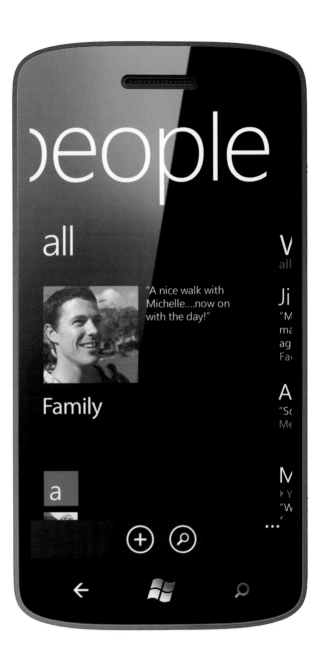

Groups

Creating groups in the Windows Phone People Hub allows you to separate your contacts into easy-to-manage groups. You could have one group for your family, for instance, another for your work colleagues and one for your Wednesday night football meet-up.

Setting up a group is easy; simply follow the steps below. We'll also explain how to delete a group as well.

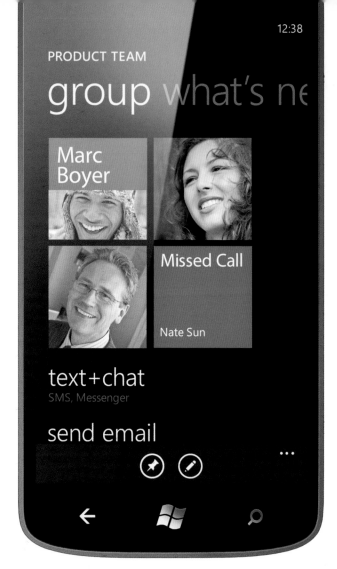

Creating a group
- From the Start screen, tap the People tile
- You should be on the All section. If not, swipe across until you find it
- Tap the plus (+) icon at the bottom of the screen
- Type in a name for the new group, such as 'Family' or 'Colleagues'
- Tap Add a Contact
- Scroll through your contacts and tap the contact you wish to add
- Repeat stages 5-6 until you have filled the group with all the contacts you want to include
- Tap the save button at the bottom - it looks like a computer disk.

How to edit a contact group
- From the People tile, tap the group you wish to edit
- Press the edit button at the bottom – it looks like a pencil
- From here you can rename the group, add more contacts, remove contacts and edit the preferred contact information for a contact within the group.

Deleting a group
- From the People tile, tap the group you wish to delete
- Tap the ellipsis icon (which is the picture of three dots in a row ...) at the bottom of the screen
- Press Delete
- The phone will request confirmation. Press Delete again.

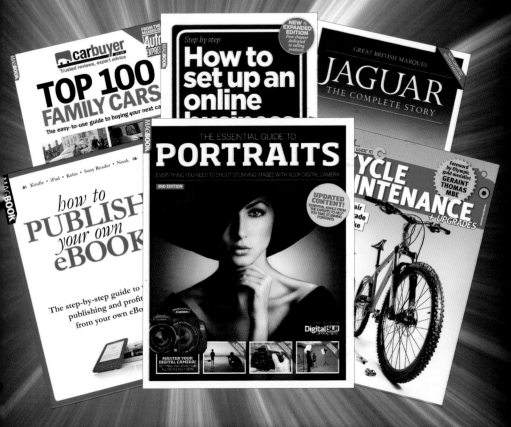

Threads

T hreads for Windows Phone takes messaging to a whole new level by blurring the lines between text messaging and instant messaging, offering users the freedom to switch between the two on the fly.

To take full advantage of Threads you'll need to set up a Facebook account. To do this, navigate to your Windows Phone's Settings and enter your Facebook details. Once you've done this you'll be able to switch seamlessly between SMS and Facebook IM inside a conversation.

Once you've done this, you'll no longer be limited to simply having a conversation via SMS or an Instant Messenger – you can have the best of both worlds. And best of all you get all this without having to switch applications. It all takes place within the context of a single conversation.

Here's a real-world example of just how useful Threads can be. Say you're chatting to a friend on your PC using either Windows Live Messenger or Facebook Chat, but then you have to leave the house. Usually this would mean the end of your conversation – but not with Threads.

Threads will let you pick up that conversation where you left off via SMS or a Facebook Chat/Windows Live Messenger IM Session on your Windows Phone handset, meaning you'll miss fewer conversations and have more freedom to chat while on the go.

Here's how Threads work on Windows Phone:

■ On the Start menu, select Messaging
■ Once inside Messaging, select Threads and then New
■ Click Add, and then scroll to the desired contact
■ Next tap Phone Number, Facebook or Messenger to determine how you want to send the message
■ Type your message and click Send

Please note that you will need to be signed in with both your Facebook account and Windows Live ID to use Facebook Chat and Messenger services in Windows Phone.

Set your Status in Threads

You can also update your status via Windows Phone's Threads as well. Here's how:

■ Go to Messaging
■ Select Threads and then go to Status
■ Select a status on the Set chat status screen
■ To see if any of your friends are online, flick across to Online and see who's available
■ Click on a contact in the Online list to start chatting.

Switching between Text and Chat

Switching between Text and Chat – SMS or Facebook Chat or Messenger – couldn't be easier. All you have to do is click the Switch button to toggle between SMS or IM. Your conversation, however, will remain inside one thread.

Send a Message using your voice

Speech in Windows Phone lets you send messages, such as texts and emails, via voice commands only. And it's pretty accurate as well. Here's we'll show you how to send a text message via Speech.

■ Click and hold the Start button
■ Wait for Speech to kick in
■ When you hear 'Listening...' say: 'text [insert the name of a contact here]'
■ Dictate the message
■ Click Send.

Pictures

Who's

add a caption

In Pictures you get access to all your snaps via camera roll, the ability to create groups for stuff and view all your online albums, as well as peruse your friends' latest image-related posts on Facebook, Twitter and LinkedIn.

The Pictures Hub is divided into a number of sections: Picture Collection, Favorites, What's New and Apps. You flick through these by swiping left. The 'What's New' section is where you can view friends' latest photo updates on Facebook and Twitter.

'Apps' gives you access to a whole number of third-party after-effect applications from inside the hub. So if you've taken a snap and want to add an effect to it, all you need to do is swipe left to Apps and download the desired effect. You can then edit the image to your heart's content.

Personalising your wallpaper

Windows Phone lets you assign different images as wallpapers inside the Pictures Hub, which really lets you personalise things. Here's how it's done:
- Once inside the Pictures Hub, tap More
- Select either the Shuffle Background or Choose Background option. Shuffle Background will automatically display random images from your Favorites folder, while selecting Choose Background lets you pick an individual image.

Share an image or video

Taken a great shot or video and want to share it on Facebook? Here's how to do it:
- Find the image or video you want to share
- Select More or tap and hold on the thumbnail
- Select Share. You should now be presented with a list of social networks
- Select the one you want and upload the picture.

Tagging friends in images

With Windows Phone, you can now tag people in your photos before you post them to Facebook. It's a cool feature and one that's extremely easy to do:
- On the desired picture, select Who's this?
- Next, choose a contact or type a tag
- Should your phone not detect a face, tap Add tag and do it manually.

Share a photo's location info

Sharing a photo's location information means that other people on your social networks can see where the image was taken. Another cool advantage of sharing this type of information is that you can map your pictures using Windows Live Photo Gallery and Bing.
- Go to Settings
- Select Pictures + camera
- Turn on Include location info in pictures you take
- Turn on Keep location info on uploaded pictures, if you want this information to stay with your pictures when you upload them to Facebook or SkyDrive

Commenting on your friends' pictures
- Interacting with your friends' uploaded pictures is a breeze with Windows Phone's Pictures Hub. To post a comment, follow these steps:
- Go to Pictures Hub
- Swipe left to What's New?
- This should bring up all your contacts' latest images
- To comment on an image, simply tap on it to open it and add your thoughts in the box below.

Social networks

Facebook, Twitter, Windows Live Messenger and LinkedIn are now pretty much an integral part of most people's lives. For instance, when was the last time you checked Facebook or posted a tweet? It was probably less than an hour ago, right?

Whether you're a social-networking addict or merely interested in the occasional tweet and Messenger conversation, Windows Phone is the operating system for you.

Featuring software-level support for all the major social networks, Windows Phone puts you in complete control of your Facebook, Twitter, LinkedIn and Windows Live accounts – and all without the need for bespoke applications. Everything takes place inside the People Hub.

To make sure you get the best possible social-networking experience on your Windows Phone it's worth signing in to your accounts when you first set up your handset. Fortunately, this is very simple, as we'll explain here.

Setting up Facebook
- From Start, go to Settings
- Select Email + Accounts
- Select Add an Account and pick Facebook
- Enter your Facebook log-in details
- Select Sign In
- Select Yes to link your Facebook and Windows Live ID

Setting up Twitter and LinkedIn
To set up support for both Twitter and LinkedIn for Windows Phone, so that you can tweet and post things to your LinkedIn account directly from your handset, simply follow the same steps as above (Settings > Email + Accounts > Twitter > Sign In)

Posting stuff to your social networks
Support for Twitter, Facebook, LinkedIn and Messenger is hardwired into your Windows Phone, so there's no need for separate applications. From inside your Windows Phone you can check-in using Bing and share your location, post Status Updates and reply to message that you've been sent in Twitter, Facebook and LinkedIn.

Posting your status
- On the Start screen, select the Me option
- Type your Message or Update and then select either Facebook, Twitter, LinkedIn (or all of them if you wish)
- Click the Send button.

Comment on a friend's status
- Go to People Hub
- Flick to What's New?
- Find an update you want to comment on, and press Comments

Checking in on Facebook and Windows Live
- From Start, go to Me
- Press Check In
- A list should appear; pick a link from the list
- Select Save.

Share a link from Internet Explorer
- Open Internet Explorer
- Find the page you want to share
- Press More > Share page
- Select Social Networks, then Post to each account you want to share it to
- Click Post

Replying to tweets
- Go to People Hub
- Find a tweet you want to respond to, and click either Reply to message or Retweet the message.

Email and linking your inboxes

As you'd expect, Windows Phone is fully kitted out for all your email needs, supporting Hotmail, Exchange, Yahoo Mail and Gmail out of the box. Other clients are supported as well, and can be set up via POP and IMAP protocols.

This native support means you get as close to a desktop experience as possible on your Windows Phone, complete with advanced search capabilities. Windows Phone scans the subject, body, senders and receivers, as well as your calendar and contacts.

Windows Phone also supports a variety of mailbox types. You can have a unified email where your Gmail, Yahoo, Exchange and Hotmail all come in together. Or you can have one for each – the choice is always yours.

Linking inboxes

Say, for example, that you want to link your Gmail and Yahoo inboxes (personal) but keep your Exchange email (work) separate. Normally this would be a big ask – but not with Windows Phone.

To link two or more inboxes together, follow these steps:
- Go to the Start screen
- Select an email client
- Tap More and then select Link Inboxes
- In the Other inboxes list, select which ones you want to link
- Now, select Rename linked inbox, type in a new name and you're done.

Unlinking inboxes

Unlinking inboxes is just as straightforward as linking them, so there's no need to worry should you change your mind. To unlink an inbox, simply follow these steps:
- Select the Linked Email Account
- Press More
- Go to the This Inbox list and select which accounts you want to unlink
- Press Unlink.

Pinning content to the Start screen

Windows Phone lets you 'Pin' things to your Start screen. This means you take a something from inside the operating system – such as a contact from the People Hub, for example – and create a shortcut for it on your handset's Start screen so you can access it quickly in future.

To create a shortcut for one of your contacts, follow these steps:
- Go to your People Hub
- Find the desired contact
- Hold down on the contact until the option Pin to start pops up
- Click it and you'll now see a dedicated Tile for that contact on the Start screen.
- You can pin as many of your favourite contacts to the Start screen as you like.

It's not just contacts that can be pinned to the Start screen: lots of other stuff is supported as well, which means you can create shortcuts for anything from Google/Bing searches and Wikipedia pages to eBay listings, SkyDrive libraries and Office documents.

Here's how to pin an app and a website to your Start screen:

To pin an app to the Start screen
- From the main menu either swipe from right to left on the touchscreen or press the right arrow button on the top right of the interface. This will take you to the Apps menu
- Once you're in the Apps menu, select and hold the app you want to pin
- Select Pin to Start.

Pin a website to the Start screen
- While viewing the website you wish to pin, tap the ellipsis icon (the three dots) in the bottom right corner
- Scroll down and select Pin to Start.

Moving a tile
- Press and hold the tile then drag it to a new location
- Tap the tile and it will slot into place.

Removing a tile
- Press and hold the tile
- When it lifts from the background, tap the icon that displays a pin with a line through it – it should appear in the top right corner of the tile.

Chapter 5

Xbox LIVE

Game on!

Whether it's a spot of green pig vanquishing in Angry Birds or subverting a deadly terrorist plot in Splinter Cell, mobile games are incredibly engaging, perfect for passing the time and, most important of all, great fun.

Windows Phone comes with Microsoft's Xbox LIVE gaming service built in, which means you have more than just access to a selection of games. You have a community you can share your experiences with, achievements to collect and a Gamerscore to show just how good you are. You can even stay in stay in touch with your friends on Xbox LIVE via the messaging service.

There's also an area called Spotlight, where you can see tips and tricks on your favourite games, find out the deals of the week and see what

Did you know?

Xbox Live has over 35 million players around the world.

games have just been released on to the Windows Phone Marketplace, all from within the Xbox LIVE hub.

Getting started with Xbox LIVE

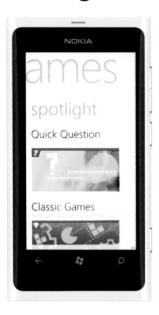

Setup

If you haven't used Xbox LIVE before, setting up your account is very straightforward.

1 On your Windows Phone Start screen, press the bright green tile called Xbox LIVE
2 Click Join Xbox LIVE and follow the on-screen instructions. Here you will be able to choose your Gamertag, the name by which you will be known on Xbox LIVE
3 If you already have an Xbox LIVE account, select Sign in and enter your sign-in details.

Creating an avatar

Once you have an Xbox LIVE account, it's time to make your avatar. An avatar can be a digital version of yourself or based on a person of your choice. It can be a serious image or something silly – it's completely up to you. The important thing to remember is you can change your avatar at any time, so you won't be stuck with it.

Xbox LIVE has a huge number of avatars from which to choose, so you can almost guarantee your avatar will be unique. Want to wear a Special Ops military outfit, look like a professional skier or have your own virtual pet dog? It's easy, as we'll explain:

1 From your Windows Phone Start screen, press the Xbox LIVE tile
2 Press Customise avatar
3 Select Change my style. From here, you can choose from a selection of pre-loaded items
4 If you don't see you like the look of, click on Marketplace at the bottom of the screen to view items you can buy.
5 Once you've made your choice, press the item you want. Repeat the same steps until you've chosen all your items. You can spin your avatar around to get a better all-round view by swiping on the screen
6 Press the Back button and select Change my features
7 Once again, work your way through the eyes and eyebrows, hairstyles, ears, nose, chin and mouth, face,

body size and colour until you are happy with how your avatar looks
8 Assuming you have an avatar you can be proud of (or laugh at), hit the floppy disc icon at the bottom of the window to save it. There's only one to press, so you can't miss it
9 If you're still not happy, select the three dots at the bottom right of the screen and press Choose new avatar to start the process again or go back to the part you aren't happy with.

Shopping for your avatar

When you were customising your avatar, you may have stumbled across the avatar Marketplace. From here you can search through thousands of different items to give your avatar a personal touch.

At the top are four featured games, together with their items. Below that is an option called All styles, which is where you can browse through everything. If that's a bit daunting, you can also browse the avatar Marketplace with the Game, Life and Popular selections at the bottom.

Top Tip

You don't have to spend money to get hold of items – some things can be won by playing certain Xbox games.

Adding Microsoft points

If you found an item you like, you will now need to add some Microsoft points to buy it, if you don't have any already. These points are Xbox LIVE's virtual currency and form the basis for all purchases.

You can buy Microsoft points in a number of ways:

- Direct from Microsoft online
- Over the counter from high-street video game retailers such as Game or GameStation, and from other high-street stores, such as HMV
- Online retailers such as Amazon or Zavvi can send you a card by post or email, which you can use to redeem your points.

These points are available in specific amounts, so you'll usually have to buy 1,000, 2,000 or 4,000 Microsoft points, depending on what you want to purchase.

Online retailers are often the cheapest suppliers, but the drawback is that, unless the redemption code is sent by email, you'll have to wait for your points to arrive. Buying direct from Microsoft is a little pricier, but the transfer is instant.

Once you've added your Microsoft points to your account, you can buy as many items as you like until you run out of credit. Most items are relatively cheap, so you can get quite a few bits and bobs for 1,000 points, but not everyone will want to pay real money for virtual items, which is understandable. The main

Top Tip

You can animate your avatar in the Xbox LIVE hub by pressing it. Keep pressing to see lots of different animations or swipe left and right quickly to see it fall over!

Did you know?

The current world record-holder, Stallion83, has a Gamerscore of over 705,000.

thing to note is you don't have to part with any money if you don't want to.

What is my Gamerscore?

Whether you're playing games on your Xbox 360 or your Windows Phone, you can receive points for completing certain challenges to show friends and family how good you are. For instance, completing a racing track under a certain time limit or not taking any damage in a fight rewards you with 10 Gamerscore points, which are then added to your overall score.

You can't use Gamerscore points to buy anything – it's not to be confused with Microsoft points – but most of the challenges on Xbox LIVE games are fun to finish, and the bigger your Gamerscore is, the more you can show it off!

The best Xbox LIVE games

Angry Birds

Angry Birds has a TV series on the way, it's a drink in Finland and there's even talk of a film, but it was the mobile game, now on Windows Phone, that got the ball rolling.

The game is simple, yet addictive. You catapult a range of our enraged feathered friends towards structures made of wood, stone and glass, in an attempt to kill pesky egg-stealing pigs. Each bird type has a different ability, which means it takes more than just luck and a good shot to smash your way through the defences, and you only have a certain number of birds to accomplish each level. The challenge is to make each shot count and achieve a three-star rating on every level.

Angry Birds is incredibly easy to play but, like the best games, it can take an age to master, which is probably why it's been downloaded over 700 million times since its launch in 2009.

If you're looking for the best Windows Phone games, Angry Birds should be on your list.

Top Tip

If you get stuck on a level, there are plenty of videos available online to show you how to get three-star ratings.

Fruit Ninja

If you went around in real life brandishing a ninja sword and slashing up fruit it would probably raise a few eyebrows. Luckily, you can fulfil any fantasies you have of chopping up melons with a sharp blade in Fruit Ninja for Windows Phone.

Fruit Ninja is a return to old score-based video games. For every fruit you slice and dice with precision swipes of your finger, points are awarded. Not everything has a positive effect, though. Bombs will put an end to your fruit-slaying days if you slice through them.

It's messy and definitely won't count towards your five-a-day, but Fruit Ninja is addictive.

Jet Car Stunts

Jet Car Stunts is all about driving a jet-powered car over obstacle courses that are floating in the sky. It's a mad premise for a game, but who wants realism when you can jump through the air in a car Batman would be proud of?

Each level in Jet Car Stunts has an objective. Usually, it's get to the end as fast as you can with the fewest number of crashes as possible. That's easier said than done, though: you have to time your jumps carefully, and coming in to land takes some skill in the use of your air brakes .

The game requires a reasonable amount of practice to master, but the feeling of satisfaction in finally beating a track will be as big as the jumps you had to negotiate.

Jet Car Stunts is an incredibly fun Windows Phone game, and perfect for those quick moments of gaming.

Civilization Revolution

Sid Meier's Civilization is an epic award-winning series that's been around on other platforms for some time, and now it's come to Windows Phone. This classic strategy game involves building an empire and conquering enemies.

Each level works like a board game. You and your opponents take it in turns to decide what you will research, build or conquer. Once you have performed your move, the enemy gets its turn to have a go. This means you can take as long as you like to plan your strategy.

As your society grows, you can start researching new technologies. You can also choose a military route, but this will be at the detriment of your ability to generate wealth.

Splinter Cell Conviction

In Splinter Cell Conviction, the hero Sam Fisher is attempting to get his daughter back from a corrupt secret agency. The odds are stacked against him, but luckily Sam Fisher is no ordinary chap – he's a highly trained Special Forces Operative with plenty of experience in the field.

Whereas many games rely on all-out attacks, Splinter Cell is about picking your fights and operating in the shadows to avoid direct conflict. You can choose to blast your way through hordes of enemies if you wish, but you will usually be heavily outnumbered. It's best to 'mark and execute' your targets quietly, and if you are seen, use cover to avoid incoming enemy fire.

With 11 3D environments to explore and tons of weapons to try, Splinter Cell Conviction is an engrossing game.

Top Tip

Download Xbox LIVE Extras and you can customise your avatar on the go, whether you want to change your outfit or try out a new hair colour.

Ilomilo

Ilomilo isn't a conventional puzzle game. Ilo and Milo are two friends who always seem to end up being separated, and it's your job to reunite them.

They live in a surreal world of colour and blocks, which makes getting them back together trickier than you may think. Blocks can be walked on at any angle and moved around, making it hard to negotiate, and you also have to collect tiny hidden creatures called Safkas in each level.

It can leave the mind boggled, but it's worth persevering with as the reward is a mini-story of the two cute heroes and the satisfaction of winning. Factor in a joyful soundtrack and the result is a game that feels good.

Available exclusively for Windows Phone devices from the Marketplace, Ilomilo should certainly be added to your collection if you enjoy giving your brain a workout.

NOKIA MAPS

details reviews

Nokia Maps

★ ★ ★ ★ ★

0 ratings

Nokia Maps helps you to be a local anywhere you go. See where you are and discover places nearby in a snap.
show details

Publisher: Nokia Corporation

update

Chapter 6

Out and about

The great outdoors

One of the great things a Windows Phone device gives you is the freedom to make more of being out and about. The latest mapping technology means you can easily find new places to go while on the move, whether you're travelling on foot, in a car or using public transport. There are also apps to help you get fit and stay up to date with the latest sports news when you're on the go.

Microsoft's mapping product, Bing Maps, provides all your location-based information. Although it's not the largest search provider, Bing is by no means inferior because it's more about local search. After all, why do you need to know where to get a pub lunch in Leeds if you live in Somerset?

If you own a Nokia Windows Phone device, you also get Nokia Drive and Nokia Maps as an added extra. Nokia Drive is designed as a satellite navigation app, while Nokia Maps is rather similar to Bing Maps. Then there's Nokia Transport for finding out the best way to get somewhere using public transport.

Obviously the weather can have a large bearing on your travel plans, and in the UK it's often a good conversation starter, too. Windows Phone is more than equipped to ensure you have a brolly about your person when the heavens open up or sun cream for the three days a year of sun we get.

You may not realise it, but your Windows Phone device is also the ideal companion if you want to get healthy. There are apps out there that can track your training, and some will even give you the option to take the scenic route to work instead of sitting on a hot, crowded train or bus.

Whatever you need or wherever you want to go, Windows Phone is designed to make your life easier.

Bing Maps and local search

Search functionality is divided into a number of areas, the first of which is the Bing Search button. Because all Windows Phone devices are the same – whether they're made by Nokia, HTC or some other manufacturer – you always press the search button represented by a magnifying glass found at the bottom right of your device. This button can be pressed at any time, so it's always just a touch away.

Once pressed, you'll see the current Bing photograph. At the top is the Bing search bar, and this is where you can search for specific results. Pressing anywhere in the white area (where it says Search the web) will bring up the keyboard. Type in your search term and press enter. Alternatively, you can press the microphone on the right to speak a search query. Speaking as clearly as possible will help with accuracy.

The first search results you see will have come from the web. Here you can browse through the first results and, at the bottom of the window, you can press to see the next results or click on the selection that bests fits your criteria.

Alternatively, if you're looking for an image, swipe left to see

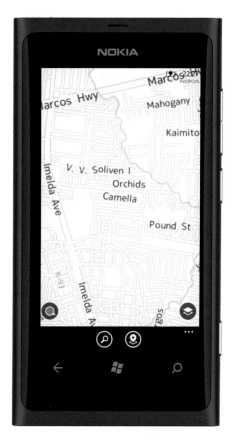

the results. Press on each image to see a larger version.

Finally, scroll to the left again to the local results. Here you can see if there's anything nearby that may be of help. So if you were looking for antiques, for example, the local antiques shop would appear, complete with directions to get there.

On that note, if we step back to the first Bing menu, you can press one of the four buttons at the bottom of the screen. The first deals with Local Scout, a search-based function of Windows Phone designed to find places nearby. The next button gets your phone listen to a song to identify who it's by, and if it's on the Zune Marketplace, you can proceed to buy it and download it straight away. The next button is designed for scanning QR codes, Microsoft tags and barcodes. It can even take pictures of text, which can then be translated, which is handy if, say, a French menu is proving a little difficult to translate and all those overly expressive hand gestures aren't helping.

The last of the four buttons is another shortcut to the Microsoft Tellme voice feature. Press it, speak your search term and your Windows Phone will do the rest.

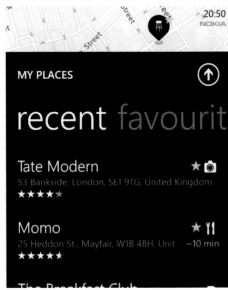

Nokia Maps and Nokia Drive

I f you own a Nokia Windows Phone, you can make use of Nokia Maps and Nokia Drive. Using Nokia's own mapping technology, it's possible to view the nearest places of interest by pressing the Places button (the middle of the three at the bottom).

You can now browse the map by swiping with your finger and zoom in by pinching the screen. To zoom out, use a reverse pinch. Just as with Bing Maps, you can search for a place by pressing the on-screen magnifying glass (not the hardware search button). If Nokia Maps can find what you're looking for, it will display it on the map along with an overall rating based on reviews.

Nokia Drive is a unique app. It provides turn-by-turn satellite navigation for when you're travelling on foot or by car. Once the app is loaded, you'll see a view of where you are. Press the bottom right of the screen to bring up the Navigation Options. Here you choose your destination, which involves either searching for a place or entering a postcode. Alternatively, you can choose to look at previous destinations to find somewhere you travelled to recently.

After entering the destination and confirming the journey, you're now good to go. Just put the phone somewhere in plain sight in either portrait or landscape fashion; it works either way.

On the screen you will see your arrival time, the route ahead, how far until your next turning and your current speed calculated by GPS. The plus and minus buttons at the top of the screen can be used to zoom in or out of the map. You can also use pinch-to-zoom to get a closer or further look at the journey ahead or just areas of interest nearby.

There's no button to return to the journey if you enter the map movement mode, but a quick press of the Back hardware button will bring back the directions.

If you go back into Navigation Options, you will see the option to swap between a 2D (top-down) view and a 3D (where the landscape is at an angle). From here, you

Top Tip
You can fully zoom in with a quick double tap anywhere on the map.

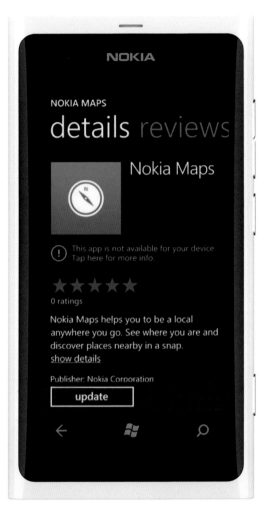

can press Settings to change the map colours from day to night and vice versa. You can also turn landmarks on or off, turn on a speed limit warning, change the navigation voice, swap between miles and kilometres, clear your search history and turn connection and location on.

For going abroad, you can download a number of maps for free. Hit Manage maps and then the plus at the bottom.

Select the country and the specific region (or all of them if you wish) and wait for the download to finish. You will need to be connected to Wi-Fi to download the maps, so you'll need to get them before you set off.

And that's it for Nokia Maps. It's very easy to use and will get you home in no time. We've tried a number of journeys using it and never had any issues with at all.

Top Tip

Ensure you've enabled Location Services in Settings and that you have a data connection, otherwise you won't be able to use Nokia Maps.

Local Scout

As we touched on earlier, Local Scout is a handy tool for finding what you need in your local neighbourhood. Simply press the search button to bring up Bing, hit the first of the four buttons and you'll be in Local Scout mode.

You should see a list called eat+drink. Local Scout will list all the nearest restaurants, each of which can be selected so you can find out more details such as the distance it is from you and the type of food that's served. That means you can choose a restaurant, press the address to plot a route via Bing Maps and phone ahead to book a table or check the opening hours, all on your Windows Phone.

You can also swipe right to check out any reviews of the restaurant to see what other

★ Top Tip

Zoom in far enough on a map and you can see aerial photos, which can make finding your way around a lot easier.

people thought of it, which could save you from a bad meal. You can also use the pin button to make a quick shortcut on the Start screen, share the place with a friend using email or messaging and add it as a favourite for faster access in the future.

Also under Local Scout is see+do, found by swiping right. This feature gives you a list of the nearest places of interest in order of proximity. Press any

of these and you will see the address, directions how to get there, a phone number and any other data Bing Maps has. You can also check out users' reviews and see if there are any apps on the Marketplace related to the search result that could be useful. As with eat+do, you can pin locations to the Start screen, share them or make them a favourite.

Next up – swipe to the right once more – is shop. As the name suggests, this is where you find your nearest shops and details on them such as opening times, directions how to get there and other information. Each section is laid out in the same way so it's instantly familiar once you've used Local Scout a few times.

In Highlights, you can see Bing recommendations in order of importance, plus any places you've chosen as a favourite.

★ Top Tip

To see local search results on a map, press the map at the top of the screen. This can help you find your bearings!

Weather apps

The climate can be unpredictable in this country, but a good weather app on your phone means at least you'll be prepared. Windows Phone has a multitude of weather apps available, and many of them can be used as Live Tiles, allowing you to check the forecast simply by glancing at your Start screen. Here are some of our favourites

Weather Flow

Weather Flow gives you temperatures throughout the day, as well as the current temperature, the chance of rain and the wind speed and direction. You can add multiple places, and accessing each one is done by swiping left or right - it couldn't be simpler.

We can't guarantee it will be entirely accurate, but the presentation is top notch, it's easy to use and the ability to pin forecasts to the Start screen is a welcome bonus.

Weather

You don't need to pay for a weather report if you don't want to. Weather, which was developed by Microsoft, is free to download and should provide all the weather knowledge you need.

You allows you to check humidity, current and future temperatures, a UV index and a forecast for the next few days.

Like many other apps, you can pin a particular city's weather forecasts to the Start screen for quick future reference.

Sky News

The Sky News app gives you a latest weather forecast in the form of a video. It's dependent on when Sky News updates its forecasts, but the video forecast is unique.

WeatherMaster

WeatherMaster does pretty much the same thing as Weather Flow,, but it does have a unique feature: its weather map. Here you can look at cloud coverage and the temperature where you are in a easy-to-read format.

If you select a place, you can add it to your preferred list so it's easier to access in future.

Rounding off WeatherMaster is another great example of a weather Live Tile. A free trial version is available so you can find out if you like it.

Health and fitness apps

Whether you're constantly struggling to keep in shape or you're a confirmed fitness fanatic, the Windows Phone Marketplace offers hundreds of health and fitness applications to help you stay healthy. Some do so by giving you incentives, others help you monitor exactly how much effort you're putting in. Whatever the method, your Windows Phone can help in your fitness fight

Endomondo →
Sports Tracker

Endomondo Sports Tracker is an app designed to track your activities using GPS. This means you can find out how far you've travelled each workout, whether you're cycling, running or kayaking (just remember not to drop your phone in the water!).

Every session you do is recorded, with an average time and your route stored for later perusal. There's also audio feedback to keep you on track while you're exercising.

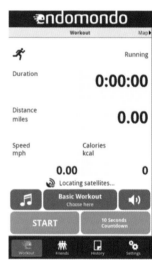

← iQuit!

Smoking is a difficult habit to kick, but iQuit! can at least help you and your determination overcome the difficult road to freedom from cigarettes.

The app won't nag you every time you spark up, but it will give you information on how much your body has recovered over the days, months and even years after your last cigarette.

If that isn't enough an incentive, iQuit! also provides information on the damage smoking can do, including how many cigarettes you've smoked in your lifetime.

170,000+ Recipes ⊙

Making the effort to exercise and become more active is the first step in making yourself healthier, but your diet also plays a large part in making sure your body is happy.

The problem is that nobody likes going on a diet. Indeed, the term 'diet' makes it sound a short-term answer. It's better to start cooking lots of healthy new recipes, and what better way to find them than with 170,000+ Recipes.

As the name suggests, this app boasts a huge library of dishes to choose from, and it can base a meal around the ingredients you have. A handy feature to help is RecipeScan, which lets you take a photo of a recipe and add it to the app.

If you're in need of some inspiration in the kitchen, the 170,000+ Recipes app comes highly recommended.

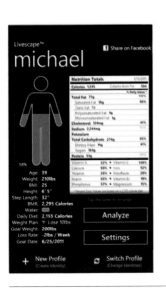

⊙ Livescape

Livescape offers a complete solution for getting healthier. It combines nutritional information with GPS tracking to help you keep an eye on your activities.

The app can also help you track your weight, calculate the number calories you burn each workout, count how many steps you've taken and set you up with a weight plan.

Livescape rounds off its range of fitness functionality with the ability to import nutrition facts using your Windows Phone device's camera, saving you from entering the details yourself.

Headphones for exercising

Music can really help you keep your spirits high and your legs pumping, which is why it's worth investing in some headphones if you plan on being active. Besides helping with motivation, headphones can also provide you with a way of making calls without having to stop - although being out of breath might make it difficult, so here's our pick of the bunch.

Sennheiser CX 300-II £34 (amazon.co.uk)

These earphones may lack a microphone or a remote for volume control, but their sound quality is unrivalled for the price, making them the perfect accompaniment to a Windows Phone even if you don't plan on using them when you're exercising.

Sennheiser technology means sound quality is great, and a two-year guarantee provides peace of mind should anything go wrong.

JVC HA-EB75-A/B/S
£6.40 (amazon.co.uk)

JVC is well known for its audio equipment, and its range of sports headphones doesn't disappoint. The HA-EB75-A/B/S set produce high-quality sound with plenty of bass.

It comes with adjustable clips to ensure they don't fall off. They're also splashproof, which may help if you get a bit sweaty from all the exercise!

With three colours to choose from and an iPhone-compatible cable in the box, this is a great buy.

Sennheiser PMX 80 Sport Mini
£6.40 (amazon.co.uk)

When playing sport, you don't want anything coming loose. The PLX 80 Sport Mini's useful backband means these headphones stick to your head.

The out-of-ear design also means you can hear what's going on around you – an essential safety precaution if you're running or cycling near traffic.

Sporting apps

Sports fans need never miss any of the action again, as Windows Phone enables you to watch the big match on your mobile – so no matter where you are in the world, as long as you have a data connection you can catch up with all the latest action

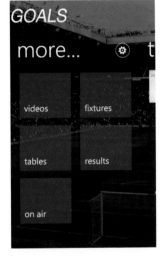

Sky Sports News

Few names are as well respected in the world of sport as Sky Sports. It's become the home of football, cricket, golf, Formula 1 and boxing, among many other sports. Now you can keep up with the latest scores and transfer gossip with this Sky Sports News app.

It boasts video content in many forms, including video interviews, reactions to the biggest stories and exclusive coverage of sporting events.

If that's not enough, you can also check out fixtures and see all the latest results and news in a brief round-up.

ESPN Goals

If you want to watch every Premier League goal almost as soon as it's been scored, the ESPN Goals app is for you.

This excellent free app includes live scores and video highlights of each game as well as the goals.

As if that wasn't enough to keep your eyes firmly on the game, ESPN Goals also includes alerts to let you know when a new video is available to watch, so you don't even need to be using the app to know there's new coverage to watch from the Barclays Premier League.

Top tips to make your phone last longer

Windows Phone devices are very power-efficient out of the box, but you can do a few things to prolong your phone's battery life.

One of the biggest drains on battery life is location services. It's vital when using Bing Maps or Nokia Drive, for example, but if you're just sending emails or playing games, do you really need it on? Chances are, probably not. Location services can be switched off under Settings, which can be found on the Start screen or in the app drawer. Just remember you've turned it off, though; some apps that use it won't prompt you to switch it back on again.

Screen brightness is another battery drain. Having your phone on the brightest setting is great to look at, but it's not always necessary. At night-time, for instance, a low or medium setting is sufficiently bright. The Automatic option decides what setting to use based on how bright your surroundings are, but choosing the medium setting is usually good enough, and it noticeably improve battery life. Brightness can also be found under Settings.

It may seem obvious, but some tasks – such as checking how many new emails you've received or fast-forwarding a track when playing music – can be done from the lock-screen. It may not save much battery power, but at least you can lessen the time you have the Start screen glaring at you.

Windows Phone Mango added a very useful feature designed to help save battery life. Under Settings, you can find something called Battery saver. When your Windows Phone has just 10 per cent battery life remaining, it will automatically turn itself on to stop a number of services and help you make it to a plug in time. You can turn the setting on before, though, if you really need to keep as much battery life as possible.

When your phone is in Battery saver mode, emails won't be synchronised, so you'll need to refresh your inboxes manually to see if you have any new messages.

If you really need to keep your Windows Phone going and can't get near a power socket, avoid checking emails or playing video, music or games, as these all deplete the battery.

Chapter 7

Photography

Snap happy!

Nokia has a fantastic history when it comes to mobile photography, with the company snatching pretty much every camera phone award going for its Nokia N8 Symbian device.

However, the company's latest Windows Phone devices take this expertise to an entirely new level, and include more fine photography features than ever before.

Nokia's three range-topping devices – the Lumia 710, Lumia 800 and Lumia 900 – all feature stunning cameras, giving crystal-clear results every time.

The Lumia 710 has a 5-megapixel camera, while the 800 and 900 both sport an 8-megapixel camera with a Carl Zeiss lens. $\rightarrow$

Choosing a camera phone

If you're in the market for a new phone you can also use as a camera, there are a couple things you need to consider. A camera's ability doesn't rely on megapixels (more megapixels just allow you to print out a massive picture), but how it senses detail and light. The lens is also a very important factor, and Nokia's Carl Zeiss lens is a great example. You should also consider buying a camera phone with image stabilisation for crisp shots.

What's a Carl Zeiss lens?

The Nokia Lumia 800 features a Carl Zeiss lens, something you're more likely to see in a digital SLR or compact camera than a smartphone.

Carl Zeiss helped to revolutionise the world of photography in the 19th century, producing lenses with very high aperture – first for microscopes and then for cameras.

Today the company produces lenses for many of the world's largest camera manufacturers, including Hasselblad and Rollei medium format cameras and Leica, Canon and Nikon digital SLRs.

Top tips for better photos

Composition

Composition applies whether you're using an SLR camera or your mobile to take pictures. The horizon and any other important focus points in your image should sit a third away from an edge. It's tempting to put the subject in the centre, but this can make the picture look unbalanced.

Choose the right mode

Windows Phone devices support a range of different photography modes, including Macro, Landscape and Night. When you select one of these modes, your camera will automatically change the settings so you get the best results.

Focus

Always remember to use the focus option. Most Windows Phone handsets support 'touch to focus', meaning you can touch the screen where you want it to be the clearest. You'll also be able to press the hardware shutter button halfway down and it will guess what you want to be the main subject in your photo.

Watch your light

Make sure the light source is highlighting the subject, not behind it. Also, try to use natural lighting rather than the flash. In most situations the flash is too harsh.

Mobile camera accessories

If you're going to take photography seriously on your Windows Phone, you'll need some accessories to keep up with compact cameras. Here are three essential add-ons for your mobile camera.

Hama Handy Mini Mobile Tripod £9.79 (amazon.co.uk)
Although many phones have a stabilisation setting, a tripod will ensure your pictures are always perfectly clear, wherever you are. The Hama Handy Mini Mobile Tripod has been specially constructed to hold your phone, and will ensure your landscapes, portraits, wildlife shots and party shots are all perfectly in focus, even if you don't have a steady hand.

Jelly Camera Phone Filters $15 (around £9, photojojo.com)
Always wanted to capture that extra bit of detail? Photojojo's Jelly Camera Phone Filters allow you to do just that, and also add a colour kaleidoscope and starburst effects to your photos. The reusable filters just stick on to your phone, and are small enough to fit on your keyring so you always have them with you.

Polaroid PoGo Digital Photo Printer £39 (amazon.co.uk)
If you want to do more with your photos than just send them to Twitter or Facebook, Polaroid's PoGo Digital Photo Printer allows you to print out your pictures via Bluetooth. It's about the size of a phone and uses Polaroid's Zero Ink printing paper, meaning there won't be a mess left behind after printing your photos off – and you don't need to buy new cartridges.

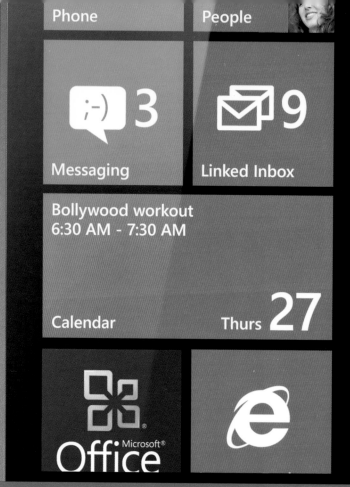

Chapter 8

Work smarter with your Windows Phone

The Office hub

All work and no play may have negative connotations, but many of us have to work on the move. Windows Phone's Office hub is exactly what you need for this, providing you with the ability to create, edit and send Microsoft Office documents.

Press the Office hub tile on the Start screen and you'll be taken to the OneNote page. Press the plus button to add a new note or press the All button to see all your OneNotes. If you want to see the most recent note instantly, it appears as a tile below.

The next page in the hub is Documents. From here you can see recent documents, explore Word, Excel or PowerPoint and create a new document from scratch by pressing the new document button.

Once you've selected this, you can choose to create either a Word or Excel document. Select Word, and you'll be presented with a text display and an onscreen keyboard. You can type here as you would normally, but there are a few other useful options.

If, for example, you leave the document and swipe once to the right, you'll see the Locations screen. From here, you can view documents on your phone, on Office 365, SharePoint or SkyDrive. We'll explain more about these – as well as many other features – over the next few pages.

OneNote

OneNote is a place where all your notes sit, whether you want to remember what to buy at the supermarket or need to remember an important point from a meeting. You'll find it in the Office hub.

Reminders you set up in OneNote synchronise with SkyDrive without you having to do a thing, so you know they'll be wherever you go. You can add a voice note, a to-do list or any other list and send any of your notes in an email. Want to add a picture? Just tap the picture icon.

To add a new note, head to Notes from the Office Hub and select New. You can just start typing your note and it will save and sync to your Office 365 or SkyDrive if you've set the services up (and set your notes to sync to both during set up). If you already have a note, select the note you want to read or add to and start typing again.

To create a new list, tap the + icon from the OneNote screen and tap on the tick icon to create a new to do list or the list icon (three horizontal lines)

to create a new general list. To add a picture, tap the icon with a plus icon in the centre (the third one along the bottom) and you'll be taken to your picture gallery. You can choose a picture from your Camera Roll, preinstalled pictures or photos from your SkyDrive or Twitter uploads. You can also choose a picture from a date or your favourites. Alternatively,

tap the camera icon at the bottom of the screen to record the current moment.

You can also record voice notes using OneNote. To do this, simply tap on the microphone icon at the end of the toolbar when you're creating a new note.

To format your notes, tap on the three dots for more options. Here, you can choose

to add a numbered list, indent lists and format the text by underlining it, making it bold, italicising it or changing the colour. You can also add a strikethough effect.

Your finished notes will all be ordered in notebooks, which you can view by tapping the notebook icon in the centre of the window that appears when you launch OneNote.

SkyDrive, Office 365 and SharePoint

Microsoft supports three different services when it comes to storing your files on Windows Phone. Although you can save documents and files on your smartphone, you may find it a better option to save them in the cloud, so you can access them wherever you are, whether you're on your phone, your home computer or in the office

SkyDrive

The SkyDrive service allows you to upload and save documents to your very own cloud space so you can access them wherever you are.

Your SkyDrive can be shared with others, and if you use the official Twitter app for Windows Phone, your pictures will be shared via the service.

Once you've set up a Windows Live account (see page 22 for more information), you can access your files directly from your phone or from a web browser on any computer at skydrive.live.com.

SkyDrive allows you to create Word, PowerPoint and Excel documents, too.

If a file is too large to send to friends, family or colleagues, just send them the link for the file on your SkyDrive. They will then be able to view or download the document securely, without you revealing your login information.

Microsoft Office 365

Microsoft Office 365 is a service provided by Microsoft that allows you to access your calendars, email, shared documents and web apps wherever you are.

Just as you can with SkyDrive, you can create and edit Word, Excel and PowerPoint documents using the cloud, but with Office 365 you can also access your calendars and email.

With 10GB of storage included in the package, you can upload important documents and share them with colleagues, clients or anyone else securely.

Video conferencing allows you to host calls and show presentations to people around the world, and the ability to share desktops means those in the conference call can see what you're talking about.

SharePoint

Microsoft SharePoint is an enterprise service that allows a company to share information, documents and reports in a secure environment.

Windows Phone supports the SharePoint service, allowing you to access everything from your phone.

You can share documents using a Wi-Fi connection or your phone's data connection and it's easy to access, right from the Office hub.

To access your locations, select SharePoint, then Locations. If your Windows Phone is already logged into the account linked to your work's Office 365 account and you use SharePoint as part of the package, you'll see your team site as an option. You can then enter the URL of the SharePoint site and access all documents, information and reports from one place.

You may be asked to sign in, in which case your phone will try to use your Exchange email details. If this isn't the correct login information for your SharePoint site, you can enter your details manually, using either your Office 365 details or your login details for your SharePoint site. Just enter your username and password, followed by Domain and type in your domain name. For example, if you log on as domainName/kevinc at work, you'd type domainName without kevinc – this should be your username.

You should now be able to browse everything you can see from your office's network.

Email

All Windows Phone handsets will feature Microsoft's Outlook Mobile email client. It works in almost exactly the same way as Outlook on your PC, but is a more cut-down version of the program.

Outlook Mobile allows you to set up a variety of accounts from a range of email providers on your Windows Phone device.

It also includes in-app support for multiple Microsoft Exchange accounts, so you'll be able to check your all corporate and work email.

Within your email app on your Windows Phone device you can search for specific emails, reply to invitations straight from your inbox and perform mass-deletes, which gives you the freedom to know that you'll always be on top of both your personal and professional life.

Within Windows Phone 7 you can also flick through your emails one by one simply by pressing the arrow keys. If you find one you no longer need,

tap the dustbin symbol and it will be deleted.

Alternatively, if you receive a message that you want to mark as extremely important, well then you'd better flag it. To do this, simply press the Options key and then select the desired location. Easy.

The Outlook email app is designed to make life easier for you. It achieves this by displaying your emails across the app's panoramic backdrop in four sections:

■ **All** – this is your full inbox (or at least all the emails synced with your phone)
■ **Unread** – this is where all your unread messages are, so you never accidentally miss one.
■ **Flagged** – here you can flag or assign important emails so they remain in view and don't get hidden under any other messages.
■ **Urgent** – this is similar to the Flagged section in that, if you receive a very important email, you can send it here and it will remain there until you delete it.

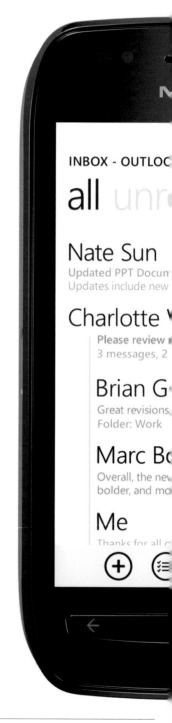

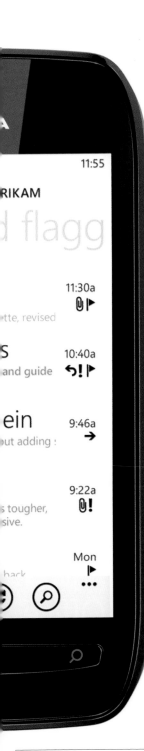

11:57

CONVERSATION
3 of 3, 2 unread

Charlotte Weiss

Please review revised brand guidelines
Tuesday, 05/10, 10:40 AM

To: David Alexander; Chris Hill; Marc Boyer
Cc: Brian Goldstein; Nate Sun

Show all recipients (5)

🔒 Protected message

https://Fabrikam.sharepoint.com/brandguide

Calendars

C alendars are commonplace on smartphones, but the Agenda function on Windows Phone can do much more than simply show you what you have on when.

The calendar function on Windows Phone can be found in the apps list (swipe once from the Start screen), but you can also pin it to your Start screen for faster access.

The calendar connects with your existing Exchange or web-based email account to ensure you have all your appointments at your fingertips.

This means that whether you use Exchange, Gmail, Windows Live or any other email service with calendars, you can be assured your phone will always be up to date.

Just as you can add multiple email accounts, so you can add multiple agendas, too.

If you have a number of different email accounts set up on your phone, you can either view a unified calendar with all your appointments colour-coded according to which email account they're linked to, or view your different calendars

as separate entities by swiping your finger across the screen.

If you've organised a meeting or accepted a meeting request at a specific location, you can view the destination on a map. If you're not sure how to get to the meeting, you can also pull up detailed turn-by-turn instructions that will guide you to your location, just like a satnav.

You can send a meeting request to any of the contacts in your phonebook or email all attendees of a meeting, straight from the calendar application.

If you're running late, for example, send the message to everyone due to attend the meeting. It also means you can send round meeting notes to all attendees without even opening your email application.

You can also send a meeting request to any of your contacts from the calendar in Windows Phone 7. Just set a date, enter the time and location and select the recipients.

Any appointments you add to your calendar will sync with your computer-based email account so you'll never be late or miss a meeting again.

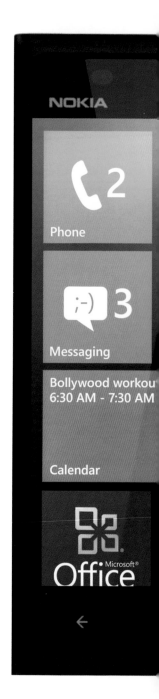

Surf faster with Internet Explorer

Windows Phone features the Internet Explorer web browser built in, allowing you to surf the internet easily. Here are our top tips for getting the most out of the browser on Windows Phone

Tap to zoom in

By double tapping on text or a picture, you can zoom in so you can see it better. You can also pinch to zoom in, making browsing on your phone an intuitive experience.

Share links

If you want to share a link via email or text, just press and hold the link and tap Share link. You can choose whether you want to text the link, send it via email on any of the accounts set up on your phone or share via a social-networking site.

Top Tip

Turn your phone around to landscape mode to see web pages in full screen.

Share a picture
Just as with links, you can share pictures from web pages by tapping and holding an image. Choose the option to Share picture, or save it to your picture library to send later by selecting Save picture.

Make a call from your web browser
Microsoft's Internet Explorer browser allows you to call people straight from the browser. If you've searched for a company from the browser, just tap on the highlighted phone number to call it or the address to navigate to it.

Add a new tab
Unlike many mobile browsers, Internet Explorer on Windows Phone allows you to have multiple tabs open at the same time. Just tap on the three dots to access the More menu and select Tabs. Tap the + icon at the bottom to add a new tab.

Pin a website to the Start screen
You can add your favourite websites to the Start screen by tapping the three dots (the More menu) and selecting Pin to Start. A website shortcut will appear on your Start screen as a screenshot of the site.

Did you know?
According to StatCounter, 34 percent of the world's population uses Internet Explorer to log on to the World Wide Web.

my kind of phone
The official Windows Phone UK blog.

Twitter

From earlier: On the blog: Going out this weekend? Don't leave home without this Windows Phone app http://t.co/n3Xnv65r

POSTED 7 HOURS AGO

Going out this weekend? Don't leave home without this Windows Phone app

Heading out this weekend? Whether you're hitting an art gallery, a DJ set or a...

POSTED APRIL 26, 2012

Discover what fans of Windows Phone are saying and add to the conversation

★ ★ ★ ★ ★ 5 / 5

about

Windows Phone brings your contacts, messages and pictures together in one place, making it easy to share life with the people you care about most, keeping you in touch and always up to date.

Search... 🔍

→ news

→ apps & games

→ customer reviews

→ wishlist

→ music

→ stuff we like

get social & subscribe

Follow us online for the latest news, tips and competitions or subscribe to our newsletter and blog

Chapter 9

Other resources

Taking it further

icrosoft's Windows Phone might be young but it's already achieved a lot. There's the award-winning Metro UI, for instance; the multitude of ways to search with Bing; and, of course, all those awesome bolted-on extras such as Zune Pass, which gives you unlimited access to millions of tracks online. And that's just the software.

Windows Phone devices are available from a variety of big-name manufacturers, including Nokia, HTC, Samsung, LG and Dell. Blending style and substance, these handsets are modern, designed for today's world and future-proofed with cutting-edge technology.

Nokia's Lumia 800 with Windows Phone (see page 11), for instance, has been receiving praise all over the world for its gorgeous design, excellent performance and built-in free services such as Nokia Drive and Nokia Maps (which are now available on all Windows Phone handsets, by the way, thanks to Nokia).

The Windows Phone Newsletter and Blog

N ow you have your Windows Phone device, you'll probably want to ensure that you're always up to date with what's going on in the ecosystem – you never know when the next big thing's going to happen with Windows Phone. Everything moves so fast.

A good way of keeping in touch is to sign up to the Microsoft Windows Phone Newsletter, which will keep you in the loop for everything Windows Phone-related. If something exciting is happening – such as the next big Windows Phone update, or a new game release from EA or Rovio – then you'll be one of the first to know about it.

To sign up to the Windows Phone Newsletter for regular updates, simply go to www. windowsphone.co.uk and follow the instructions.

If you've signed up for the Windows Phone Newsletter but you find you can't wait a full week for your dose of Windows Phone news, then you need to check out www. mykindofphone.co.uk.

Pulling together all kinds of user-generated content – including reviews of handsets, apps and games – the My Kind of Phone blog is the only place you need to be for everything Windows Phone.

Inspired and built with Windows Phone's Metro UI in mind, the My Kind of Phone blog features six distinct

sections: News, Apps & Games, Customer Reviews, Wishlists, Music and Stuff We Like. Each section of the blog is updated every day and there's a thriving community of users on-site to chat and share hints and tips with.

You can also submit a review of your Windows Phone to mykindofphone.com. You'll notice the reviews are extremely positive, with many people happy to recommend Windows Phone. If you're loving your mobile, then why not tell the world about it?

Whether you're look for a new Windows Phone handset or just a new app or game to download, your first port of call should be the My Kind of Phone blog.

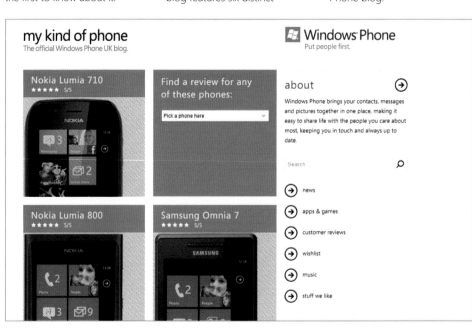

Become a fan on Facebook

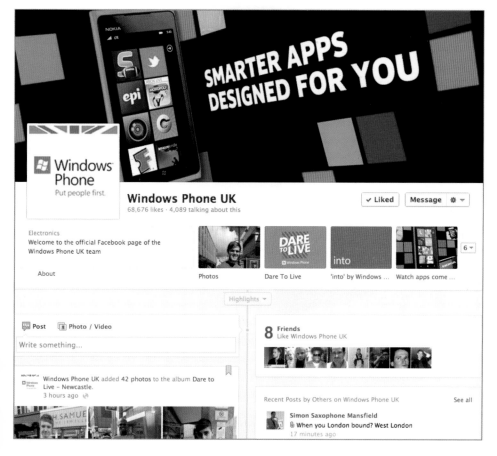

ecoming a fan of Windows Phone on Facebook is yet another way to stay constantly updated with what's going on in the world of Windows Phone. There are more than 68,000 people on there to connect with, links to cool videos and up-to-the-second news updates from the Windows Phone team.

If you're after real-time updates to go alongside your Windows Phone Newsletter subscription and regular visits to the My Kind of Phone blog, then becoming a fan of Windows Phone on Facebook is the way to go – who knows, you might even meet some new friends as well.

Windows Phone is also on Twitter (@WindowsPhoneUK), which is handily built into your People hub so you can see all the latest tweets from Windows Phone and all the other people you follow. Keep your eyeballs peeled for T-shirt Tuesday and Freebie Fridays, too – these happen on a regular basis to reward loyal friends and fans of Windows Phone.

To see the latest and greatest videos from Windows Phone, head to the YouTube channel (youtube.com/windowsphoneuk), where you can watch Windows Phone taking on other smartphones in the Dare to Live challenge, learn how the Windows Phone apps come to life and view handy how-to videos.

The Ultimate Guide To Windows Phone

Editor Clare Hopping

Contributors
Richard Goodwin, Ben Griffin

Production Editor Steve Haines

Art Editor Nik Byrne

Digital Production Manager
Nicky Baker

MAGBOOK

The MagBook brand is a trademark of
Dennis Publishing Ltd, 30 Cleveland St,
London W1T 4JD. Company registered in
England.

MANAGEMENT
MagBook Publisher
Dharmesh Mistry

Operations Director
Robin Ryan

MD of Advertising
Julian Lloyd-Evans

Newstrade Director
David Barker

Commercial & Retail Director
Martin Belson

Chief Operating Officer
Brett Reynolds

Group Finance Director
Ian Leggett

Chief Executive James Tye

Chairman Felix Dennis

LICENSING & SYNDICATION
To license this product, please contact
Carlotta Serantoni on +44 (0) 20 79076550
or email carlotta_serantoni@dennis.co.uk.
To syndicate content from this product,
please contact Anj Dosaj Halai on
+44(0) 20 7907 6132 or email
anj_dosaj-halai@dennis. co.uk.